Praise for

"Want to know what the real le
here." - Carl Ledbetter, SVP &

"Priceless wisdom from experts
business objectives." - Frank Campagnoni, CTO, GE Global Exchange
Services

"A wealth of real world experience from the acknowledged industry
leaders you can use in your own business." - Doug Cavit, CTO,
McAfee.com

"A quick and comprehensive view of the key challenges and
outlook....by the some of the best in the business." - Satish Gupta,
CEO, Cradle Technologies

"Get real cutting edge industry insight from executives who are on the
front lines." - Bob Gemmell, CEO, Digital Wireless

"An unprecedented collection of best practices and insight..." - Mike
Toma, CTO, eLabor

"A snapshot of everything you need to know about the
industry/profession." - Jack Guedj, President, Tvia

"True insight from the doers in the industry, as opposed to the critics on
the sideline." - Steve Hanson, CEO, On Semiconductor (NASDAQ:
ONNN)

"Unlike any other business books, Inside the Minds captures the
essence, the deep-down thinking processes, of people who make things
happen." - Martin Cooper, CEO, Arraycomm

"The only useful way to get so many good minds speaking on a
complex topic." - Scott Bradner, Senior Technical Consultant, Harvard
University

www.Aspatore.com

Aspatore Books is the largest and most exclusive publisher of C-Level executives (CEO, CFO, CTO, CMO, Partner) from the world's most respected companies. Aspatore annually publishes a select group of C-Level executives from the Global 1,000, top 250 professional services firms, law firms (Partners & Chairs), and other leading companies of all sizes. C-Level Business Intelligence ™, as conceptualized and developed by Aspatore Books, provides professionals of all levels with proven business intelligence from industry insiders – direct and unfiltered insight from those who know it best – as opposed to third-party accounts offered by unknown authors and analysts. Aspatore Books is committed to publishing a highly innovative line of business books, and redefining such resources as indispensable tools for all professionals. Aspatore is a privately held company headquartered in Boston, Massachusetts, with employees around the world.

Inside the Minds

The critically acclaimed Inside the Minds series provides readers of all levels with proven business intelligence from C-Level executives (CEO, CFO, CTO, CMO, Partner) from the world's most respected companies. Each chapter is comparable to a white paper or essay and is a future-oriented look at where an industry/profession/topic is heading and the most important issues for future success. Each author has been carefully chosen through an exhaustive selection process by the Inside the Minds editorial board to write a chapter for this book. Inside the Minds was conceived in order to give readers actual insights into the leading minds of business executives worldwide. Because so few books or other publications are actually written by executives in industry, Inside the Minds presents an unprecedented look at various industries and professions never before available.

INSIDE THE MINDS

INSIDE THE MINDS:
Leading CTOs
Industry Visionaries Share Their Knowledge on the Art & Science of Technology

Published by Aspatore Books, Inc.

For information on bulk orders, sponsorship opportunities or any other questions please e-mail store@aspatore.com. For corrections, company/title updates, comments or any other inquiries please e-mail info@aspatore.com.

Third Printing, 2003
10 9 8 7 6 5 4 3 2 1

ISBN 1-58762-056-1

Library of Congress Card Number: 2001119342

Cover design by Michael Lepera/Ariosto Graphics & Kara Yates

Material in this book is for educational purposes only. This book is sold with the understanding that neither any of the authors or the publisher is engaged in rendering legal, accounting, investment, or any other professional service.

This book is printed on acid free paper.

A special thanks to all the individuals that made this book possible.

Special thanks to: Jo Alice Hughes, Rinad Beidas, Kirsten Catanzano, Melissa Conradi, Molly Logan, Justin Hallberg

The views expressed by the individuals in this book do not necessarily reflect the views shared by the companies they are employed by (or the companies mentioned in this book). The companies referenced may not be the same company that the individual works for since the publishing of this book.

The views expressed by the endorsements on the cover of this book for the Inside the Minds series do not necessarily reflect the views shared by the companies they are employed by. The companies referenced may not be the same company that the individual works for since the publishing of this book.

INSIDE THE MINDS:
Leading CTOs

*Industry Leaders Share Their Knowledge on
the Art & Science of Technology*

CONTENTS

CLOSING THE GAP BETWEEN WHAT TECHNOLOGY CAN DO AND WHAT PEOPLE WANT IT TO DO

DR. CARL S. LEDBETTER

Novell

**Senior Vice President,
Chief Technology Officer**

The Role of the CTO

CTOs get to help make the future, and most often they do that by explaining what technology can do. I'm a scientist by training, education, and nature, but my background for that is probably a little unusual. I was a philosophy major throughout most of my college years, and my family upbringing wouldn't have suggested a career in technology. My father was a minister, a preacher – and a very scholarly one, the kind who had degrees in ancient Greek and Hebrew and church history. His sermons, which I listened to every Sunday until I left home for college, were always on abstruse, arcane subjects out of the Bible, such as the translation of a particular word from Hebrew and how it applied to the topic of his sermon that day. Interestingly, though, about midway through every sermon I ever heard him preach, he would depart briefly from his scholarly presentation to perform a magic trick in the pulpit. The tricks were all different – I never saw the same one twice – and each of them illustrated by some kind of a topical reference the point he was trying to make in his lesson, something that made the very technical, intellectual, academic subject come alive in a visual way that people would remember. The result is that his congregation was always packed, and people were sitting on the edge of their seats until he did his trick.

What that taught me, almost intuitively, instinctively, is that the way you make difficult subjects clear to lay people is by using analogies, stories, and references to things they know and understand. If you amuse them, entertain them, make them laugh, you also make them understand what's important, even if what matters is otherwise very difficult, complicated, even beyond ordinary understanding. In my case it's technology I'm trying to explain, rather than religion (and I note that my subject is far easier than my father's), and the task is to render accessible to lay audiences what is technically difficult – to show them the heart of the matter as it applies, or will apply, to their lives and interests, without resorting to all the techno-babble that many technologists in the industry fall into instinctively. Such mumbo-jumbo obscures the real issue behind technical language you don't really need to know to understand the main themes in the evolution of technology and what it can do. So because of that lesson my father unknowingly taught me, I have always stood with one foot pretty comfortably in the technical arena and the other in what you'd have to call marketing – by which I mean the ability to explain what the technology is about, how it works, why it's important, and how to use it in a way that doesn't require the listeners to have a Ph.D. to understand. I look for ways to do that and admire it when someone else does.

For example, recently I was in Toronto at a huge conference on e-government. E-government is a catch-all phrase for how you use the computer and the Internet to interconnect everybody to everything they want or need to do with the government. Canada's vision is quite stunning; they call it "One Window, No Wrong Doors." You log onto the Net and go to Canada. You want a fishing license, you get a fishing license; you want a driver's license, you get a driver's license; you want a passport, you get a passport. It's a matter of indifference to the citizen that the fishing license is issued by a local jurisdiction, the driver's license by a province, and the passport by the Canadian federal government. The Canadian government realizes the citizen shouldn't need to know which jurisdiction is responsible for which government activity – it's likely even the government can't keep it straight. So Canada's idea is a wonderful concept, but even better is that they would present this to Canadian citizens in the "One Window, No Wrong Doors" format. This invites citizens to come to the Net to work with the Canadian government, without confusing the issue with a lot of unnecessary complications. This approach says, "Just look in the window the government provides, and we'll get you to the right place, even if you're not a computer expert." So when I went to Canada to explain Novell's role in this new way of thinking about the Net and how Canadians will be able to use it for government services, I needed a way to make this approach clear without being overly technical.

My way of explaining how this would happen, being faithful to the technical potential without exposing all its complexities, was to take up a Rubik's Cube. (I actually wrote the solution book to that more than 20 years ago.) I tossed the Cube into the audience and had people scramble it up, and then during the course of the speech, I solved the Cube in front of them, using it as a prop to make clear how a hard problem can be broken down into easy-to-understand-and-execute phases, and then I tossed it back at the end of the speech completely restored. I doubt that anybody will ever forget the demonstration, but more importantly, they will remember the parable. What I did was a way of saying, "Here's why it's hard. Here's how you attack it. Here's how you do it." If you attack the Cube in some random fashion, you're never going to solve it – it would take you, on average, 1.8 billion years to finish it if you did it that way. And learning the technology – the mathematics of group theory – to solve it on your own is a daunting multi-year effort for math majors. But we solved it in considerably less time than the speech, of course, and the analogy to how Canada can solve the problem of creating e-Government access for all Canadians within four years was clear. I joked that I wouldn't take too long to solve the Cube because I didn't want them to miss lunch, and their politicians didn't want to take too long to provide Net access to the Canadian government because they didn't want to miss reelection.

Overcoming People's Intimidation by Technology

People are intimidated by what they don't understand, and more so if they believe that what they don't understand is important to their success. The difficulty in getting people to feel comfortable around technology is what C. P. Snow called the problem of two cultures – for him these were the scientific and the literary cultures; they would probably be better described as the technical and the non-technical now. The real issue is that scientists and engineers think things are important if they're technically interesting. But most people think things are important if they're useful. And those are not the same thing at all because frequently being technically interesting means being inaccessible to those who are not technologists.

When I became president of the consumer division of AT&T, one of the first things that happened was that someone from marketing brought me an ad they had been working on before I arrived, something they were very excited about. The advertising agency was coming to show me this wonderful new creative piece to get the buy-in from the new president of the division. The ad was part of what AT&T called the "You Will" campaign. It was a vignette of someone on the beach, holding a computerized slate, similar to what we would now call a PDA. The ad said, "Have you ever received a fax from the beach?" And the tag line was, "You will." My answer to the ad executives was, "Gee, I hope not."

What that ad did was confuse what we can do technologically with what we want to do in real life. Why in the world would you want a fax from your boss at the beach? The issue is not technical; it's sociological. What exactly is the protocol when your boss wants to get you, when he knows he can reach you, when he can even confirm that he has reached you, that you have the message, but you won't answer him? You're on vacation. You don't want that fax. What exactly do you say to him? What's your excuse for not responding? There has to be a sociological convention for this; having the technical capability to send faxes to the beach is not the same thing as wanting it to happen.

If you look far enough back in time, you can find an industry that has gone through the phase we're in now in the computer industry, and beyond it, so you can see the effect. Look at the turn of the century – the last one, the early 1900s. The automobile industry was at a nascent stage; it had some interesting things going on, with Ford Motor Company, in particular. I often ask technical audiences when I'm giving speeches to engineers, "What's the most important invention in the history of the automobile industry?" And I get all kinds of interesting answers: internal combustion engines, independent suspension, automatic transmission, radial tires, even tubeless tires sometimes if someone is really thoughtful about what was going on back then. But I think the answer is none of those, and it's not limited slip-differential or fuel injection, either.

The most important technical inventions in the history of the automobile industry are the electric starter and the enclosed cab. Those inventions meant you didn't have to be an engineer or a hobbyist to use the car anymore. Because of those innovations, the wives of the hobbyists (they were almost all men then) could, and would, ride in the car. Because of those innovations, the automobile was transportation instead of engineering. Only when you didn't have to crank the stupid engine outside to get it started – you could push a button to make the machine run, and then get inside the relatively comfortable cab to go somewhere – was the car useful, and therefore interesting, to non-engineers; the electric starter made the automobile accessible to the masses. Because they could ride inside the cab, where they wouldn't get their hair blown into a mess by the wind, the automobile became comfortable to use for ordinary people, rather than a hobbyist's plaything. In other words, it wasn't a really big technical breakthrough that made the automobile industry economically successful, and it wasn't a technical innovation that made it acceptable for large groups of non-technical users – it was something that made the car easy to use for the average person.

The most important insight I think we've had today in the technology industry is that our computers are plenty capable enough technically; they're just so damned hard to use that they're infuriating! I've been using these machines since 1970-something – before my kids were born, and they're 22 and 20 now. I used to think that every good software development kit had a soldering iron in it. But even I can't do that anymore. If I install some new software application, or some Microsoft upgrade, or a new system utility on one of my machines, everything breaks for weeks. I just can't stand it.

We cannot have that if we hope to take the industry to the next stage. The most important thing we have to understand about what will happen in the technology industry is that we will be successful only when we stop designing things for engineers – we have to start designing them for my mother.

I started taking PCs home to my mother about ten years ago. I set the first one up for her, so she could do e-mail with her six kids – I got her a PC, a modem, an ISP connection, and the right software, and made sure it worked, showing her how to use it to send e-mail. She was delighted. But after a few days or a couple of weeks, I'd stop getting e-mail from her, and when I'd go back to visit, every two or three months, the thing was out in the garage. "What's the problem?" I'd ask. "Well, I was using it just like you said, and I got this blue screen, and something said I had a 'fatal error,' so I figured it was dead, and I put it away." All she knew was that it didn't work anymore, and she didn't have a clue how to fix it. She couldn't use it. The instruction manuals were useless – they were a foreign language to her and didn't tell her what she needed to know to bring the machine back to life. "I can't even understand the Table of Contents or the Index," she said. "How can I figure out what to do?" And it's not that she's stupid; she's just the way everyone else in the world is, except the handful of us who are basically geeks.

When my son was about 13, it was time for him to go out and get his own first software program, one that he would buy with his own money, so I took him down to the software store for what turned into a two-hour session. He had to look at every box in the store, of course, all the games, and then he bought the one he liked best. He brought it home and put the disk in the drive (this was in the days before CDs). There was a great big, slick manual in the fancy box, and it immediately went over his shoulder into the pile of blue jeans and t-shirts, never to be seen again, and he started hammering on the mouse. I said, "Don't you want to read the instructions?" And he said, "Dad, instructions are for wimps." And he was right. That's what people do. If you can't figure it out by looking at it, you're not going to fool with it, and that's the most important lesson for technologists and engineers to learn. Even online instructions are a mistake – making instructions and help files more accessible is dead wrong; what we need to do is make them unnecessary.

I was riding in an airplane a few years ago and saw what was probably the single most important instruction guide I've ever seen – I understood what this industry's problem was in a heartbeat. I was on a flight to Europe, where they pass out those little foil-wrapped packages of lotion-saturated tissues to clean your hands with after a meal. This one was called a Wet-Nap. As I was fumbling with it, I saw the directions, which read, in their entirety, "Directions for use: Open and use." That's it. Open and use. No other instructions necessary. If we could get this Wet-Nap interface into what we do technologically, we would be winners. Almost all the innovation and brain power that will be applied successfully in the next three to five years in this industry will be used to close the gap between what technology can do and what people want it to do, and to making it easy, which is to say obvious, to use.

Defining Success as a CTO

Ultimately to be a success as a CTO, you have to make the company successful by aiming it in a direction that will be fruitful for the development of technologies that customers will want to pay for. At the end of the day, I work for a company, so I work for shareholders, and it's my job to help make the company successful. But that task is really one of choosing main directions and grand themes, to seek out the right path for a time two or three years down the road, rather than next quarter.

To do this successfully, CTOs of the major technology companies have a responsibility greater than to their own companies. That responsibility is to help the industry, the governments that regulate it, and all the other components that are associated with that enterprise aim in the right direction and think of things in the right way.

For instance, we're all now very interested in what we generically call "security issues" on the Internet. But I think that largely we worry about the wrong things. Encryption technology – the worry about whether your credit card number gets stolen – that's really not as big a problem as people generally think. The SSL link – you don't even need to know what that is, but it's basically secure server technology for transmitting your credit card number, for instance – is sufficient for most purposes. I'm not worried about handing my credit card to Amazon.com over an SSL link. I'd be a lot more worried about handing my actual credit card to the 18-year-old kid who just graduated from high school who's the waiter at the restaurant I went to last night. He can take my card to the back of the kitchen and make a rubbing of the number a lot more easily than anyone can pick it off from Internet traffic.

The real issue to consider in Internet security, for everything we do, in commerce and in the very important things that are emerging in health care and government use of records, is the privacy of those transactions and records once they are securely transmitted. Privacy is really about the management of a trade-off between the risk of giving others information about yourself so you can make things you want to do easier to do, and the risk that the information you supply in this way will be misused or abused in a way you don't want, by someone you don't intend to have it or isn't authorized to use it. This privacy issue is much more of a boogeyman than what we call the security issue.

A year-and-a-half or so ago, someone in the press found out and revealed that some Internet sites were parking special kinds of cookies on your disk. Cookies are small collections of information that are stored on your disk to remember certain things about you to make it easier to navigate and transact on the Net; they overcome the limitation of the fact that your transactions on the Net are stateless – every page, every hit is new news to the site you're on, unless there is a way to remember something about who you are, what you have done there in the past, and where you came from. Cookies are very intrusive in and of themselves, but the penalty for not permitting them is that you really can't use the Internet for most useful kinds of commerce, and even having your machine warn you when they are being parked on your disk is an unacceptable annoyance, especially when most people don't even know what cookies do or understand what accepting them means. Go look on your browser at the file that contains your cookies; you'll likely be stunned at how many are there and where they came from.

But some sites were doing worse than just putting cookies on your machine: They were also watching what you did while you were out at other sites on the Internet, collecting that information, and sending it back the next time you landed on the cookie's originating site. Horrible! They were spying on you, and they were using your own PC to do it to you, without your consent, without even your knowledge. And they were both using the knowledge about where you went for their own purposes and also selling that information to people and businesses whose sites you probably would never have visited. It was intrusion of the worst possible sort, invasion of privacy that is wholly and entirely unacceptable. Now, these companies, when caught, promised they wouldn't do that anymore, and I hope and expect that these particular sites do not. But others might, and do.

The real issue with this is that there are ways to intrude on your privacy that you would neither tolerate nor permit, if you knew about them, which can be hidden by the technology, and they are still being exploited on the Net. We have to be very vigilant about these kinds of intrusion and ensure that people are made fully aware of what is at stake.

And there are other kinds of intrusion that are, if not as explicitly unethical, at least as objectionable. There are sites that force what are called pop-ups, or, worse, pop-unders. These are windows that are spawned by an originating window you've opened, either on purpose or accidentally, and parked either on top of the original window or underneath the one you're looking at, and which may continue to generate a storm of other windows being opened, essentially taking over your machine by launching windows faster than you can close them. This technique is like nothing so much as a door-to-door salesman who not only knocks on your door to sell you something, but kicks in the door, forces his way in to your house, and trashes the furniture, even when you've told him no. The industry has to drive this kind of behavior out of existence. It's one of the few places where technology needs the government to protect users from the abuse by its misapplication.

Even the issue of "opt-in/opt-out" I find infuriating. These terms refer to the two ways that have been proposed to handle the most common of the intrusions computer technology enable, the creation of mailing lists that can be used to solicit us with e-mail. The worst offence is spamming, the widespread practice of sending out thousands, even millions, of e-mails to a long list of addresses, to solicit something, but even more targeted mailings can be objectionable. Opt-in means that you get such e-mails only if you explicitly request them; opt-out means you get them unless you explicitly tell them not to e-mail you. In my view, the opt-out approach is hideously burdensome. It's like saying anyone can force you to waste your time figuring out how to get off unwanted mailing lists. The advocates for the opt-out make the argument that opt-out is the better technology because it is better for business and is closer to the laws that permit junk mail. But, of course, consumers hate junk mail, and the analogy is flawed because there is at least a barrier to junk mail in that it is costly to produce and deliver, much costlier than the e-mail equivalent. Almost all consumers would prefer opt-in, getting advertising materials, e-mails, solicitations, information, only from sites and about subjects they are interested in and have requested. I don't mind having Mountain Tools or Black Diamond Equipment send me information on their products because I'm an avid mountain climber, and I like receiving information from them. I sign up for their catalogs; I shop at their sites; I give them certain information about myself because I want to. But I don't want to be inundated by information about insurance, how to make a million dollars at home stuffing envelopes, chain letters, and worse. That stuff is just infuriating. And it's hard, and time-consuming, to figure out how to get off their lists, and sometimes it's essentially impossible – just sending them an e-mail telling them to quit it is difficult to do and may even generate even more unwanted e-mail because sending a reply, even if it's to say Stop! has the unintended effect of confirming that the e-mail address is a legitimate one that can be sold to others. The only acceptable technology is to require opt-ins, rather than permitting opt-outs, but I predict it will be a long battle. These junk e-mails, and spamming in general, ought to be prohibited by law and excluded by technological means when possible.

Those are the kinds of issues we need to be worried about. CTOs in the industry need to make sure we're talking about them in ways that will help the government and members of society who are not technologically inclined understand what is at stake, so they can make the right choices and force the right legislation.

Exciting Technologies in the Works

I travel all over the world, and I do so, essentially, with two documents: I have a driver's license for use inside the U.S. and when I'm getting on airplanes, and I have a passport that will get me into most countries. So I can cruise across almost any border in the world, and I'm able to identify myself and transact whatever business I want when I'm traveling by using just those two documents.

When I'm on the Internet, it's a very different thing entirely. The Internet is supposed to have made the world smaller, to have eliminated borders, and to a large extent it has, but it hasn't made it much easier to do business while you're out there. The problem on the Net, as it turns out, isn't access, it's identity. I don't even have one name on the Internet. I was actually looking into this for a speech I gave recently, and I counted all the names I had in my various relationships on the Internet. I found I had 36 different ones – not different passwords, different names. Sometimes I'm Carl Ledbetter; sometimes I'd have to separate my first and last names with an underscore; sometimes I have to use a space; sometimes my names are concatenated; and on and on. I've even learned there are several other Carl Ledbetters in the U.S., so sometimes I have to use my middle initial to distinguish myself, and there are even four other Carl S. Ledbetters, so I have to use my full middle name or some other differentiator, and with all of these I have the underscore, space, concatenation issue to contend with. When it's all added up, I have so many names I can't remember which one I am

19

on any given site, especially the sites I visit only infrequently. When you add in the more than 70 different passwords I have, there are nearly 2,500 different user name-password combinations that are possible from among the ones I actually use. And the passwords change all the time, so my big yellow sheet of paper is all scratched up and hard to read. It's a wonder I can do anything at all on the Net. So I do what all of us who are concerned about computer security tell people not to do – I put the user names and passwords I use on a big piece of paper and tape it to the side of my monitor – where they can be seen by anyone even mildly interested in stealing my identity, thereby compromising the security provisions that protect me, to be able to get to those sites at all. What a nightmare.

Recently, I was trying to get on to a service that handles my kids' tuition, and it asked me for my user name, so I could check to make sure the deductions had started. I tried three or four times and couldn't get in, and then, because I had made the maximum number of attempts permitted, I got locked out. I had to make a phone call to get help at the service, and you know how harrowing a process it is to get a live person these days. That company spent a lot of money, and I spent a lot of time – and was pretty irritated while I did it – just trying to make sure I could pay my bill. How dumb is that? They made me fight to pay them money – all because I didn't know my own name on the Net. So I can't travel around the Internet the way I do around the world because I don't have the right to my own name and can't remember the information I need to authenticate my identity.

What we really need is illustrated in a great line from a movie several years ago, *The Adventures of Buckaroo Banzai Across the Eighth Dimension* – "No matter where you go, there you are." That's what happens when I travel the world with my passport: No matter where I go, there I am, and I know my name, I have credentials to transact business, and my identity can be authenticated reasonably well by whatever gate-keeping authority is checking. I want to do the same thing on the Internet. I want to be able to make a claim about my identity and to have as many identities as I want – because I may have good reason for having several different personalities or roles that I want to distinguish. I want to make sure the agency of authorization can identify me correctly and that I'm authenticated by reasonable means at some level of assurance that may vary by purpose and mechanism of authentication. And then, now that I'm on the Internet, I want to be able to move around without being pestered over and over again for the identity and authentication credentials I've already presented. From the time I'm in and authenticated, almost all the dot-coms should accept me for who I am. If the authentication is at a high enough grade – maybe just knowing my password is good enough for some purposes, but knowing other information, having a smart card, or presenting biometric information like a fingerprint or retinal scan could be required for other more sensitive and secure applications – there ought to be a secure-certificate technology that makes sure my identity and authentication, with all the rights and privileges of access I'm allowed from that, gets handled correctly and handed off as I instruct, so I don't have to do it again. My one-time authentication ought to be enough to allow me to navigate around the Internet's electronic world, just as my passport allows me to travel around the physical world.

I think the thrust of the next five to ten years will be to make that vision a reality. No matter where you go, there you are, on the Internet. The industry will create software components that make this happen without forcing customers to jump through a lot of hoops or know a lot of things.

Positioning Your Company for Change

One of a CTO's most important roles is positioning his or her company for changes that are likely to happen. The CTO is an internal evangelist, as well as an external spokesperson. You have to rally the engineers and the business people inside a company to understand the big scene: Why is this market going to make it? Why is it productive for us to spend resources in one arena, rather than another? What technology choices should we make, and what will that technology do to solve a real problem that matters, that has economic value?

There's a story that Warren Buffett used to decide which companies to invest in by listening to what products his wife and her friends were talking about – what was going on in the grocery store and at the shopping mall. That's a very important part of the issue: What is actually happening in the real world, as opposed to what technical things are the engineers interested in?

We spend far too much time looking in the mirror, thinking we're seeing the rest of the world. We're not watching what other people – non-technical people – are doing. Amazingly, technical people often argue with others about what they should want to do with technology, surely a losing argument every time it occurs. It's the same problem the automobile industry had when it was still making cars for hobbyists instead of their wives. We have to figure out how to make machines for people who don't care how the technology works.

I saw one of the most brilliant technology advertisements ever a few years ago, for a satellite TV service. It was for Hughes Direct Broadcast Satellite TV, which was one of the companies that started that whole industry. In the commercial, an actor came out and started talking about "Direct Broadcast Satellite" – using that technological word, "satellite" – but then he immediately stopped talking about the technology and asked, "You like movies? We have 250 movies, ready at any time. You like basketball games? From Gonzaga University?" When do you ever get to see Gonzaga University play on TV, except maybe during March Madness? Are you a displaced Broncos fan, living in New York, who wants to see the Denver Broncos play Seattle when they're showing the Jets against Miami where you live? With Direct Broadcast Satellite, you can use an easy little index to choose what you want to see, and you have hundreds and hundreds of choices. Then the actor said, "How do we make all this happen?" He started to turn around, and behind him, an old-fashioned green chalkboard appeared and filled up with a bunch of equations – real ones – any technologist would recognize the Schroedinger Wave Equations, Maxwell's Equations, some phase-shift calculations, things that really do matter to making the technology work – but the actor looked back at the camera and said, "I have absolutely no idea."

The supremely important subliminal message there is that some very smart people who understand this technology were back there working on this. They got it to work. But you and I don't need to know how they did it. What you need to know is that you can watch Gonzaga play basketball on TV tomorrow if you want to, or see *Gone With the Wind,* and all you have to do is push a few simple buttons.

That's the technology story we have to get to: Make the technology easy to use for people who don't care about technology, and then technology will succeed. Try to make technology for the geeks, and you'll satisfy only the geeks. The job of technologists is to make technology invisible in any application. The way to make it useful is to make it disappear from view. Almost everyone drives a car in this country, but almost no one can tell you what kind of transmission is in it. What are the gear ratios? How many quarts of transmission fluid? My point is that this is a good thing. Transmissions are crucial for automobiles. Once they were the subject of important engineering innovations on the leading edge of automotive technology. But they became most important when they disappeared from view, when they were not only automatic, but also invisible.

Taking the Right Technology Risks

With one very interesting exception, the only real judgment that can be applied to taking risks is, Will the product be commercially successful? If you're in business, you're in business to make money, and the shareholders are owed every effort to make a business economically successful so they can be financially successful. So you have to tune the technology risk correctly to get the right thing done for real customers who will want to buy the products and services you offer.

The exception to this is in the realm of public service. Often we learn a lot about how to make successful products by doing something for free in the public interest – things like the Internet grid that attempts to "Fight AIDS at Home." It is perfectly plausible that hundreds of thousands of PCs working part-time when the screen savers are up can actually find some drugs by using the molecular modeling software that pharmaceutical companies use or by searching through the genome information that's now becoming publicly available. We'll actually find some things just by brute force by exploiting the idle time of machines that are temporarily or intermittently under-employed, and I think that's a useful thing for the industry to support, endorse, and find ways to enable. But principally, companies won't be around to help in those kinds of projects unless they make money with what they do, and you make money only by finding markets that go beyond the early adopter phase. And to do that, you have to create technologies that make non-technical people capable of something economically valuable, in which the enabling technology is so good that it disappears.

Best Business Advice

When I was a young, second-line manager at IBM, I made a major presentation to my boss's boss's boss's boss on a big project I wanted funded. It was a big deal for me, and I worked a long time on the presentation. I thought it was absolutely terrific; it was slick; it was right; and it was the right thing for the company to do. But I was running against a tide I didn't really understand at the time. IBM was having a rough quarter, and there were some political issues afoot, and I couldn't get the full attention of the division president when these other things were on his mind; he was too distracted. He liked it, but he wasn't going to fund it just then because he couldn't afford to put it in the budget. So I got sent home to do some more work and more study, and come back in six months to see if we could do it then.

I was bummed out by this and probably a little surly in the next few meetings I had that day, and I was a little distracted myself. The next morning, I was a little overly curt in a meeting with my staff. My secretary at the time had been with IBM for 25 years, so basically I reported to her – she knew more about the company than I did. She had worked for a lot of very senior IBM executives on their way up through jobs like the one I was in, so she knew everybody. After that morning meeting, I went back to my office and was working on some e-mails, when she came in to ask if she could talk to me for a second. When she had my attention, she looked me right in the eye and said, "You have 120 people reporting to you. When you have a bad day, they all have a bad day. Knock it off." And then she left.

Hers was exactly the right advice. People who are in positions of leadership and authority have a duty and responsibility far beyond what they feel like personally. There's a continuity issue associated with it: Leadership requires that you stay on your game all the time. I used to joke with my wife that every time I'd go with her to the mall in blue jeans on a Saturday morning, I was absolutely certain to run into someone I knew from work. There's never a private moment, and that's an important business message. You're always on.

Managing in a Turbulent Market

I think there is an interesting sense in which people are always over-optimistic at the same time they are also over-pessimistic. I've said often that the Internet is the most over-hyped technology in the history of the world, but it's also the most under-estimated. Not only does the market swing from extreme to extreme, but also people's sense of what's going to happen swings from extreme to extreme. And there's a kind of counter-intuitive way you should manage particular technology investments because of that.

When things are just blowing the lid off, like during the go-go days of the dot-com bubble, rather than going out and hiring like crazy and making more investments in wilder and wilder things, you should start to pull back, start inspecting everything you do with a much sharper eye, start cutting back programs, and be much more skeptical about what's going on.

Conversely, when everything is in the dumps, pour on the coal. Now that the Internet bubble has burst, it's time to hit hard with investments in technology. Things are cheap. Innovation has slowed. What we do now has a better chance to win because it's not as obscured by clutter and nonsense, if we're doing smart things. You need to be counter-cyclical to the way the world thinks things are happening. This is the very best time to invest in the market. It's the very best time for venture capital, the very best time for technology.

People will be successful in this market – just not this month. But this is the time decisions are being made, technologies are being developed, investments are being placed on things we'll be talking about in three years. It doesn't happen over night. Nobody invents something as complex as the things we're working on now in an afternoon. What's being invented now will be suddenly important when they are mature, and it will look like an explosion of creativity and innovation again, but it is really happening very quietly right now.

Becoming a Technology Leader

Although I learned a lot of things at IBM that were very important, this is something I learned that was wrong, and knowing that it's wrong is one of the most important lessons I ever learned. IBM at that time had a particular philosophy of professional management. They believed that management was itself a discipline, so if you can learn to manage something well, you can manage anything well. I think that's not true. My advice to anyone who wants to be in an important role, whether in technology, or finance, or sales, or marketing, or whatever, is that within your general discipline, you need to be really good at something. It doesn't matter what it is – but you do need to be good at it, and it has to be something of substance, something that's hard to master, something that matters. You have to have earned your credentials, made your mark, gotten your stripes, from having been at the very top of some important subcategory of the discipline you're in, or else you can't possibly understand how to manage things that are on the cutting edge of the larger enterprise you're going to lead.

In my case, as a technologist, I have a Ph.D. in mathematics; I studied computer architectures; I had a very, very successful machine program at IBM; and there are other successes I've had in my career. I've earned a kind of credibility as a result of these successes, with the engineering community, both within my company and in the industry in general, that cannot be won in any other way. It's a kind of a union card, a secret handshake that marks me as a member of a certain society. When I walk into a room full of engineers, they all know who I am and what my background is. Because they know I am a technologist, they think I understand what they're talking about, even if I don't. I can ask unbelievably stupid questions as a result of that, and that's a very important skill. And I will not accept an answer that has any of the technology mumbo-jumbo or acronyms that the computer industry uses. "Enterprise application integration?" What the hell is that? I don't have a clue, and anyone who uses these terms is probably masking a lack of real understanding behind industry buzzwords. No one ever challenges those kinds of things unless they're confident they understand the technology they're working on. It's important to be good enough at something that you're not worried about looking stupid.

About 1994, I was talking to some very senior AT&T executives, trying to explain what was going to happen with IP – the Internet Protocol – and ATM – Asynchronous Transfer Mode, a cell-switching network standard – which are underneath all we do on the Net. I asserted that it would become a substitute for voice, and anybody who was going to be moving bits around on big backbones was going to get ranked into a commodity vendor, which is exactly what has happened to AT&T in the last seven years. During the course of this explanation, I was talking about the difference between circuit switching, which is the way telephone calls are completed, and packet switching, which is the way the Internet moves packets around. I said IP technology and ATM were going to be alternatives to the way telephone companies switched voice, and that was a threat to AT&T's entire enterprise because anybody who moved bits around would become a commodity supplier of pipes.

During the course of this brief monologue, one of AT&T's most senior executive interrupted me and said, "Carl, this is all very interesting, but we still don't understand what automatic teller machines have to do with telephony." He thought ATM meant "automatic teller machine," the machines that dispense cash at your bank. A senior executive in the largest telecommunications company in the world didn't know the technology that was about to clean his clock. He has since gone on to another telecom enterprise, which has failed miserably, and I don't doubt why. He doesn't get it. He didn't have enough technology–specific expertise to make good decisions or to understand what was going to happen to telecommunications technology. He might have been a great manager in another industry, but not in this one. The skills are not transferable.

You cannot understand this industry if you don't know certain things about the technology that underlies it. You don't need to rub people's faces in technology; you don't need to have the customers understand it to be successful – in fact, that would be an impediment. But you have to have that union card. You have to be credible. You have to know enough about how things work that you can make reasonable decisions about the way the technology will go. You have to be really good at something.

Keeping Your Edge

I read constantly. I use the technologies constantly. And believe it or not, I watch other people constantly. In my kids' dorm rooms in their first years of college, I watched them play with their computers, and I noticed the things they did. I noticed, for example, the rise of the Napster phenomenon and of peer-to-peer sharing of files because they were doing it. I watched instant-messaging technology because they used it and said it would be killer. The kids keep these windows open on their desktops all the time, carrying on interrupted two-way conversations with a dozen or so people at one time, while they're sitting there doing their homework. That's a very different way of thinking about the world, and unless you actually see it happening, you don't know how it works.

You have to get out of your own environment. You have to watch what real people are doing. And you have to make sure you're drinking your own brew, that you're away from people who are like you. It's sort of like the story about Warren Buffett's wife: Find out what your spouse is doing, rather than thinking that the world is like you.

In the October 1878 issue of *Scientific American,* there's a story written by a very knowledgeable science writer of that time. It was the first month after the commercial introduction of the telephone from the new American Telephone & Telegraph Corporation. The writer talked about what he and the company thought the main uses of the telephone would be. I was dumbstruck when I read it. He thought the major application of the telephone would be managers of large companies talking to their employees on the assembly line, giving them pep talks and company information. The manager would be up on a balcony overlooking the assembly line, and each of the workers would have a handset. Or people would subscribe to opera, so they could sit around the phone in their home and listen to a performance, or to the broadcast of a baseball game during which they could chat amongst themselves as if they were in the stands.

What the article missed was that telephony was a brand-new means of private two-way communication that meant that two people who were not in the same room could have a conversation no one else could hear. There was no paradigm for this at all at the time. The paradigm that did exist was the new radio broadcast technology, so this new telephony idea was inappropriately shoehorned into that format in the speculations of even pretty savvy observers. Who would have thought back in the late 1800s that there would be billions of telephones in the world today? There was no way to think of that, no experience that predicted it.

What we often miss with new technologies is their eventual real use and importance. The way to stay sharp is not by studying journals, but by watching what people do – observing the sociological implications of technological change.

The Golden Rules & Skills of the CTO

The most important skill a CTO can have is to be able to understand technology well enough that you can explain it to people without having to go into acronyms and mumbo-jumbo. You should be able to do it with metaphors and analogies in a way that makes technology clear not only to the people who are not technologists, but also to technologists who are in related areas but are not themselves experts in your specific field of reference. You should be able to give people a sense of confidence in understanding how the pieces all fit together. This is so important. It's what distinguishes a CTO as a public spokesperson from someone who is a great development manager, for instance, for software or hardware devices.

You can do those other jobs and be able to talk about XML and TCP/IP; you can't do a chief technology officer's job if that's all you can do. You have to be able to make it sing for people who don't know the tune. They may never know the words, but it's important for them to be able to hum it.

But you also have to have that union card, that fundamental indicator of credibility. Engineers love it when a technical person succeeds in business. That's why there's something approaching hero-worship of the geeks who actually make it to the top of a business enterprise from the engineering community. It's fun for them to see someone who comes out of their world succeed in a different way. But the reason some can do that is that they can find ways to articulate those technology visions that take the technology off the front burner and make it recede into the background.

As a chief technology officer, you also have to keep your head up. Go back to the 1960 presidential debate between Kennedy and Nixon. A major bone of contention in that debate was the fate of Quemoy and Matsu, two little islands out in the China Sea. The moderator posed that question, and these two guys who wanted to be President of the United States of America got down to the nits and bits about these two tiny islands – and that was the last time those islands were ever an important issue in world politics. They basically just didn't matter.

It's way too easy to get caught up in a specific, right-now contention or technical issue and get your head down into those details, with your nose in the dirt, where it doesn't matter. We CTOs have to keep our heads up, so we can see where the ship is going for the long haul. I think we too often get far too embroiled, for instance, in which standard is going to succeed, and that's not what matters. What matters is what the standard is trying to be used for, so we can figure out where the whole enterprise is going. I think the most important golden rule is to keep looking five years out.

The Future of Technology

The single most important issue for technology will be privacy because as soon as people actually understand what's happening to them, there will be outrage and a period of retrenchment and all kinds of regulations; in fact, the government will get into it in ways that we don't want them to. They'll handle it even worse than the industry does today.

Here's another important issue. Human beings are extraordinarily efficient receivers of information. Even when you're sitting around like a couch potato, watching "Ally McBeal," you're getting the equivalent of millions of bits per second because you're seeing a TV picture. We're extremely efficient machines at seeing something and picking out of it what's important, almost without any conscious effort. And we're pretty tolerant, in ways that machines are not, of moderate errors in that. For instance, if there's one bad pixel on the screen you're watching, you probably won't even notice it; you can ignore that input. So we're efficient consumers of high amounts of bandwidth because we can afford to ignore most of the data that's going into that bandwidth. This marvelous brain of ours allows us to figure out what's important and what's not.

So in five to ten years, we're going to have access, everywhere we go, to a six-megabits-per-second continuous stream of information that we can look at. We're not very good at generating information; it takes us a long time to type a document of a few thousand bits. So we don't send very much up individually, but we sure do suck a lot down. The other big technological imperative of the next decade is going to be getting the bandwidth connection secured to be able to get those six megabits everywhere we go. We'll get it wirelessly in many cases. We'll figure out ways to make the investments and to develop the right business model to get that done, so we can look at anything we want to look at, anywhere we want to go.

We bought our kids an encyclopedia when they were around six years old. My kids never looked at it. They don't even look at the dictionary. They look everything up on the Internet – essentially, the new library of Alexandria. We're going to be able to get that everywhere we go. Our kids will carry these tiny devices that will give them information they need anytime they need it, anywhere they are. Six megabits appears to be what it takes to put full-blown, razzle-dazzle, blow-your-eyes-out, full-motion graphics and video onto the device you're looking at. So getting six megabits everywhere is probably all I'm going to care about for a while. And the one piece of dream technology I really would want to help create is one that would let me get those six megabits through the air by a private subscription channel – emphasis on private. I want a completely secure, private mechanism for finding any piece of information in the world, wherever I am. It's the combination of access and privacy in a secure environment that is the greatest technology this generation will produce.

Carl S. Ledbetter is chief technology officer and senior vice president of Novell, Inc. Joining Novell in 1999, he was chief technology officer and senior vice president, Business and Corporate Development of Novell, responsible for leading Novell's move to a one-Net services approach and championing Novell's open-standards, cross-platform development efforts, including software architecture, strategic partnerships, technology evangelism, and Novell's Venture Fund.

Dr. Ledbetter's experience includes roles as chairman and chief executive office of Hybrid Networks, Inc., an innovator in the wireless broadband industry; as president of AT&T Consumer Products; as leader of Sun Microsystems's PC networking business; and as a principal of Decision Point Consulting. Before joining the computer industry, he taught mathematics at Wellesley College and Clark University, and was academic dean and professor of mathematics at California State University, Sonoma.

Dr. Ledbetter earned his Ph.D. in mathematics from Clark University, his master's degree in mathematics from Brandeis University, and a bachelor's degree in mathematics from the University of Redlands.

CREATING AND ENRICHING BUSINESS VALUE

RICHARD SCHROTH

Perot Systems

Chief Technology Officer

The Role of the CTO

The CTO is one of the key technology leadership positions in many organizations. This position can be defined in many different ways but is most commonly associated with the efforts to advance the technology of a company and to communicate the difficult task of strategic business and technology positioning. The CTO is generally seen as the key individual who helps establish or influence the next generation of technological products and services of the organization.

The title of CTO is being established in more and more organizations as the newest of the senior leadership positions, and generally the CTO serves as a direct report to the CEO. In that regard, I view the CTO as an individual who has the responsibility to help shape and influence both the strategy and processes of the organization, to enrich external client relationships and business value through the smart deployment of technology to solve business problems, and to understand the basic elements of the technology deployed by the organization, both globally and locally.

The CTO must focus on and execute three primary areas of the responsibility. First is understanding and influencing the business strategy and value system of the corporation. Second is continually trying to understand and put into conversational perspective the evolution of the technology as a whole. From this position, the CTO should be able to provide guidance to the company with that knowledge. The third primary responsibility is watching the business processes of the company, both internally and externally, and forming a directional strategy on how to introduce those technologies that will have the most profound effect on aiding in developing new business value and enhancing the business delivery process.

There can be an additional role for the CTO, depending upon the organization and the products or services it provides to the market. Directing the research labs or research activities of an organization is often a significant effort led by the CTO. This is especially true in technology product-driven companies where proprietary technology innovation is a cornerstone for the evolution of products to the marketplace.

Typically in this role, the CTO spends more attention on the science of the technology and becomes an influencing figure in the work of the laboratories and early product development cycles of the company.

Differentiating the CTO from the CIO

There are clear differences between the CTO's and the CIO's roles and responsibilities. Most of the differentiation is centered on the fundamentals of where they direct their focus, the degree of direct internal and external customer contact, and the planning horizons they hold critical to the business behavior. Typically, the CIO has the overall responsibility to manage the infrastructure of the corporation and deliver the day-to-day technical operations of the corporate needs and the applications that run throughout. Most of the time, the CIO is responsible for the telecommunications and information technologies and the operational service levels that support the entire technological functioning of the corporation. For the most part, the CIO is focused on the internal customer and the electronic linkages between the organization and its business partners.

In contrast, the CTO should be expected to contribute to a broader technology perspective for the company. Additionally, the CTO should play a key role in the overall management team of the company for helping set priorities and directions. When the CTO is an officer of the company, execution of those elements that involve technology or those processes affected by technology are all part of the purview for change by the CTO. Relative to the CIO, the CTO should clearly reflect a more definitive position on the business marketplace, the financial wherewithal and capabilities of the company to acquire or divest, a strong sense of technology's impact on the market drivers of the business, and the product offerings involving technology innovation that are going to affect the market segments in the industry segment.

While the CIO is managing the central IT infrastructure elements, and in many cases some of the application areas, the CTO is working in conjunction with the CIO to help bridge the elements of the business and the research facing elements. An active CTO has a large presence with all types of customer groups inside and outside the company's walls to develop relationships, bridge the technology to large industry plays, gain and test external perspectives, and build back into the company those linkages that connect it with the CTO's network of individuals, companies, and corporate clients.

Defining CTO Success: "The Theory of Three"

I was taught a long time ago about the three-trip/three-month/three-year theory as the most accurate tool to predict the success of the CTO. The three-trip/three-month/three-year theory is all about the relationship of the CTO to the business units of the organization and the value that they create. The theory is based on whether or not you, as the CTO, can engage an executive of the company in a project that requires you to visit three times in three months, and then repeat that frequency for at least three years to report progress of that and other initiatives. If you can go back to that same executive, or the successor, after the three-year period and share the same energy to repeat the relationship, then you are probably on the road to succeeding. If you can repeat the three-trip/three-month/three-year theory with all the divisional heads, and achieve an equally supportive relationship, then you have probably become a critical element of the executive team and would be considered a success in any organization.

It's a simple test, but it's surprising how accurate and difficult it can be. The three-trip/three-month/three-year theory sorts out a CTO's people skills, value creation and contribution methods, technical savvy, change management skills, and, most importantly, devotion to doing the best things for the company.

The Varying Role of the CTO

The concept of a CTO varies widely from company to company. The title of CTO has gone through quite an evolution and continues to evolve. Some of the traditional roles of the CTO still exist in many companies today. Thought of as the deep technology guru of the company, CTOs were sometimes scientists, engineers, or computer science specialists with skills primarily focused on product development, R&D, and possibly a few specialized application areas requiring highly notable skill sets.

Evolution has reshaped this early description and is converting the role to require an understanding of not only the technological implications, but also the process implications brought on by the use of the technology. This evolved position is one of the hardest to fill in organizations today, and the CTO perspective is one of the most sought-after – that of a combined deep understanding of business, business processes, and technology. Adding the ability to communicate to executive audiences increases the rarity substantially.

One of the key drivers of this shift in the role of the CTO is that the business process is starting to integrate more and more technological elements into it, so that it is almost impossible to differentiate the process understanding from the technological capabilities. Under these conditions, the CTO is no longer focused on the application or the technology but attempts to understand the fundamental relationships between the two and the required changes in both to move the company to the next generation of thinking. A bridge has to be developed between a division that is trying to execute a new application and the other elements that it has to go through to change its fundamental process. Some still call this reengineering. My thoughtful and learned colleague, James Champy, one of the inventors of the re-engineering concept, now thinks of it more as X-engineering.

The CTO is also playing a more active roll in the specialized areas of mergers and acquisitions. I find that strong CTOs in many organizations are clearly involved in the acquisition and merger decisions, much more so than a CIO would be. The CTOs go in sometimes as part of the due diligence process. CTOs performing in these capacities are clearly people who have networks and knowledge that can enrich the perspective and the business proposition of the deal. If the deal structure does not appear to create the business value anticipated, they may also propose relationships and alliance structures on behalf of the company. In my mind, the CTO must have the senior business executive skills to shoulder a broader responsibility for the corporate well-being.

The CTO as a Horizon Filter

As the CTO for Perot Systems Corporation, I initially look at things with two very different lenses. These two perspectives are formed around my role to provide service to the corporation and service to the clients with whom we do business.

In filtering the horizon inside the company, I believe that keeping a perspective from 18 months to two years is quite sufficient to allow the corporation the time it needs to prepare for new generations of initiatives. Even with some of the far-reaching technology breakthroughs on the horizon, most corporations will not tolerate significant planning horizons beyond that period. To accomplish longer-range initiatives such as this, I've always believed that research and development, or horizon planning, is done by facing the market, partnering with willing partners, and developing prototypes. Interestingly, real-world industry partnering and implementation can validate directionally and isolate the critical problems from more than one perspective. As you grow the products and technologies externally, and you find that the market has validated the functionality, there's always money for further research and development to take the next steps forward. Stand-alone, self-funded technology research and research and development projects are slowly fading into the distance, becoming the exception in creating business value. Open and partnered projects with longer horizons are always under enough scrutiny that they generally establish the right set of circumstances to make the project ready for the market.

The second filter for looking at the horizon is from the market's perspective. Generally, you should keep a list of five or ten technologies you think are profound. Going into an organization and asking about the most significant technologies an organization believes will affect them gives you a relatively clear sense of what they believe are truly the technologies that are affecting their business. Generally, the two lists match closely. Most of the time, one or two technologies will differ and create an opportunity to explore viewpoints.

A ready-to-go list of the "Ten Most High-Impact Technologies" is a great tool to have in many different situations. These list elements give you a place to start exploratory conversations about business initiatives and technology evolution and serve as a barometer to establish just how much tolerance an individual or organization has for the future and how their perspectives get framed. In using the "Top Ten List," you normally do not start with the list itself but try to establish a set of business conditions that represent the drivers, economic constraints, and value propositions. Once those are established, forming a perspective on how they're going to grow and how their markets will change creates the stories that are needed to frame the fantasy. (No one actually knows the reality, even though they may claim they do.) Bets with world-class "guessers" can bring accuracies up, but the market is the only final determiner of reality.

As you begin to list the technology reformations (the Top Ten List), it becomes very evident that you cannot talk about them without telling a story of some of the marvelous implications that will shift mankind's thinking. If you concentrate on the evolving physics of the technologies over the next generation of its Moore's Law cycles, the size of the shift starts to take on a new reality. But translating the physics into business opportunities is clearly one of the art forms of the CTO.

After the CTO makes these types of translations for many years, the art that actually becomes most useful is the final translation of the technologies into the improbable process changes that can appear somewhat unthinkable. Carefully, the CTO must figure out a way to translate what may seem to be almost a fictional glimpse into a story with a solid market presence and a business value proposition. Unfortunately, the dot-com companies used up a significant amount of credibility for such stories. As a result, many business leaders are exercising a significantly higher level of caution about any predictions they may have to absorb, and their energies for risking such change have dropped considerably.

The second level of screening the new horizon is to understand the relationship between the physics of the technology and the management science of the process. I have given this theory the name of "Process Physics." A basic theory about the evolution of business processes continues to perplex me but has served me well in trying to understand the change business faces on the horizon. I am firmly convinced that when I look at new technologies, I see an interaction between the physics of the technology and the business process itself. When Gordon

Moore started to evolve his Moore's Law theory, he laid out the fundamentals of the physics process pretty close to being correct. If this curve continues to track as accurately as it has in the past, we will continue to be able to capture a curve that has a high degree of accuracy in its predictive modeling. From that we can predict a lot of the availability of bandwidth, switching capabilities, or computing power. What he didn't anticipate or didn't focus on was that we would integrate those technology changes much more closely into the business process. In some ways the process itself was a function of the technology.

As a result, the technology shifts that are occurring at these exponential levels have started to push business change to occur at some form of a curve that has a direct relationship to the physics of Moore's Law. If you can isolate fundamental breakthroughs in technology that will occur at these focal points; you can begin to understand processes more completely. Process reinvention is no longer a duplication of the same business functionalities on an incremental scale, but represents a fundamentally new type of re-alignment or restructuring of the business process. This non-incremental opportunity is a direct result of the stage we see occurring in the exponential cycle of Moore's Law.

It is at this predictive juncture of physics and business that the role of the CTO gets much larger and becomes one of a process change agent. Ideally, the relationship the CTO has established with the operating divisions, as well as the staff functions of the organization and the senior leadership team, provides a vantage point for creating change in the organization. At this juncture, the role of the CTO must shift to a business strategy perspective, involving discussions among the senior leaders to begin thinking about the possibilities of change they must confront. It is also at this juncture where the Theory of Three comes into play, as trust and credibility become critical tools for organizations to make progress.

These reinventions of the company's thinking and approaches keep the company competitive and become a defining differentiator between the early job of the CTO and the new, evolving role. As time goes on, these curves will become steeper and steeper. Process has a defined relationship to the physics of technological change.

Pivotal Technologies

There are many pivotal technologies evolving in industry today, but one particular piece of work that has been evolving at the MIT media labs is of particular interest to me. What impresses me the most is not the technology, but the approach to the technology. The approach is to bundle a group of technologies under a functional theme. In the case of this particular research project, the labs have given it the name of "Things That Think."

Defining pivotal technologies under a larger functional umbrella is a significant step forward in understanding the much larger ramifications of their impacts. In this particular case, when you begin to think about the ability of items, from clothing to fixtures, to monitor their environments as well as ours, everything we have around us takes on an interesting importance. The idea that at some point those things can talk back and "think" back is going to be one of our most incredible uses of technology for getting our organizations to the next level of performance.

For example, look at something simple like a shoe that is being experimented on by a number of sports organizations, in particular the NFL. The new shoe is "wired" to provide information about performance. The ability to analyze the performance of athletes in new ways boggles the mind. Impact, speed, performance, distance, and efficiency become new vocabulary words for watching the Sunday NFL games.

Taking this work a step further, some of the biggest breakthroughs in the area of "Things That Think" are occurring in the material manufacturing groups. As of this writing, a small group at Georgia Tech was making significant engineering progress on a wireless shirt. This shirt has the capability to monitor everything from blood pressure to other types of physical features of an individual. The ability of various healthcare organizations to take advantage of such data and begin real-time monitoring of people and their conditions is phenomenal. It's the next generation of what we might expect to see in new forms of remote health care and preventive medicine. Moves like these begin shifting our organizations to more far-reaching concepts, such as "real-time" business.

The other aspect of "theme" technology is the ability to combine various types of evolving technology into an integrated concept. The wider you can find an integration concept like the one above, the better the opportunity to develop a point of view around the conceptual integration. Seeking principles that apply to the opportunity becomes the next level of task. As the principles are derived, the opportunity allows the business leaders to explore their deep concerns about highly relevant management issues that otherwise would never have surfaced. Taking the opportunity to involve the senior leadership whenever appropriate in such planning exercises also allows them to develop an evolving sense of the opportunities that technology and business may present them. This technique also allows them to begin to grasp the complexities that have a high probability of accompanying the process changes needed to support the technological capabilities.

As technology continues to evolve into more complex and efficient propositions, there is a need to ponder the end state for the foreseeable future. Two of the most interesting questions are, "How fast and efficient can we really run a business? Where do the profound possibilities of combining more information-dependent processes and the Moore's Law effect of technology lead us?"

It is at this point that my stake stands in the ground. It is my belief that this is the guidepost for filtering what's on the horizon. The primary thesis that drives my long-term thinking revolves around how companies will begin functioning more and more in real time.

Challenges on the Horizon

Many companies claim they function in real time and that they are real-time companies. From what I can tell, certain elements of companies may have closer to real-time concepts functioning, but we have yet to see the entire company and its surrounding business partners function in real-time in any well coordinated manner. An example of one strategic move that a company might make in real-time business would be to breakthrough the barrier of closing the corporate books in real time. When we can close the corporate books instantly, with accuracy and accountability integrated into the entire process, we will have truly achieved a new milestone in understanding the new directions of business process and technology.

The concept of "real-time business" has as one of its strategic drivers the active role of auditing, as well as revenue tracking, expense management, and inventory control, and all other asset and liability components of the company, so they can be reconciled at any point in time. If that ever occurs, and companies do have the capability of reporting to Wall Street their earnings information in real time, a whole new set of questions will find their way to the corporation's big investors, shareholders, and management – questions such as, "Do we want to trade our companies on an instant basis?" and "If Wall Street rewards that type of trading and behavior, what will companies do that are not capable yet of even thinking like that?" The concepts of "Things That Think" and "Doing Business in Real Time" are two of my ten biggest value themes that enable me to attempt to understand the technologies that are important to deploy both externally and internally and provide a measure for me to gauge how the horizon should be approached.

The Execution of Technology

Perfect execution of technology initiatives and an equally thoughtful effort in the creation of the corresponding business value propositions associated with the execution are the two most important goals an individual or a corporation can have when unlocking the power of an implementation initiative. As a rule of thumb for most corporations, cutting-edge technology deployed in open business environments is a recipe for disaster.

The execution has to do with the level of customer service that is both measured and perceived. Incidentally, lower levels of customer service sometimes established under SLAs never work or are always found unsatisfactory in the long run. Customer feedback (scorecards), the use of constantly monitored feedback mechanisms (dashboards) generated from the system, and employee feedback from those actually doing the work (project review and evaluation discussions) become the cornerstones of good execution and support of major and new technology.

The bottom line on the execution of technology speaks volumes over and over again that nothing less than consistent 100 percent perfection is the only acceptable way to view the development and deployment of technology. Short of this performance, almost anything can be questioned, be put down, or otherwise fall short of expectations from the user's perception. Interestingly enough, the senior executives who have grown up in an era of some of the first- and second-generation technology deployments find it toughest to bring this level of performance to the foreground and hold company performances to nothing short of perfection. Secondly, this expectation level is also required in reality as we evolve the "real-time business" because, again, a true "real-time business" has no tolerance or latitude for systems that fail, as the majority of system elements are dependent upon 100 percent uptime.

Privacy Issues

Privacy and the security of information are two of the most significant technology theme elements corporations will face in the next ten years. I think the events leading up to the September 11th bombings and the events after this willful act of terrorism will raise the level of consciousness around the world about accessed information and the information security marketplace. This will especially be true around more and more personally driven elements, such as our individual movements. When I talk about things like the wireless shirt, camera traffic enforcement, or even something as commercial as geo-positioning car navigation systems, the scary thought of "Big Brother" looms ominously in the foreground. The reality about many of these ubiquitous monitoring systems is that they all are fundamentally information tracking and monitoring tools. Unless the area of privacy is buttoned down much better than it is today, our society will never be able to evolve a certain sanity check for feeling free.

Additionally, no one knows for sure, at any time, where the information really resides, especially when it goes on the Internet. And even with all the attempts to encrypt and protect the privacy of individuals, there are many sloppy systems that have significant flaws. Unfortunately, since these flawed systems exist, records of personal information can permeate the Net without anyone's awareness once the crack in the armor is found. Global presence of networks, including the Internet, now presents surreal catacombs of places to hide and create mischief. Inasmuch as there is no guarantee that the information is riding the network in the U.S. or in any country where it might actually originate, deep and forceful laws are virtually impossible to mandate and enforce.

Protection of individual privacy is something that corporations are doing a moderate job in representing and enforcing. Generally, I believe companies that rally around the concepts of accountability and privacy protection will find that doing so will strengthen the brand more and more over the next couple of years. At this junction lies the problem of execution we just discussed. For example, banks recently have issued privacy information to their customers. The leaflets basically explain the privacy laws and how the banks will handle them, and then ask customers to decide whether to stay at the bank or leave.

People are confused. I would guess that 99 percent of the people just pick up these position statements and throw them away. No matter how we reach out to the individuals, as long as they're not being directly affected, privacy is not a high enough priority for them to read the legalese that must come with those things. But the minute they're personally affected by it, the idea that they gave up their rights raises their consciousness. It is a dichotomy right now because the information is replicated, gets sold, etc. It's just too overwhelming for people. I think the integrity of the business becomes the great and important differentiator as stories of privacy situations are told.

As another example of this position, if I gathered all of the data on how my financial providers handled my personal privacy, I'd probably have at least 15 different types of privacy areas just around my finances. I would have to read the legalese that would probably exceed 100 pages of privacy information. I can't do that. I put a tremendous amount of trust in those banks to not lie to me and to treat me in an upright and fair manner. I think the CTO of an organization has to be sure the company he or she represents is clearly conscious about the branding issue and understands that security and privacy have to be kept at the highest level of authority and conduct as possible.

Leadership

Personal integrity and a strong ethical attitude, combined with boundless enthusiasm, great business savvy, a strong understanding of finance, an unyielding respect for people, a love of technology, and a passion for free markets, create the most interesting leaders as CTOs. In my experience at the "C" level of an organization, especially around technology decisions, most decisions to go forward rely on a personal trust situation. Basically, the CEO, the leadership team, and the board need to know that you will stand with them and that you have the integrity to make your recommendation succeed. Once that level of comfort can be established, everything else seems to distribute very naturally in the organization. Leadership is about "gut checks."

I believe one of the key elements around leadership for the CTO is to be able to understand the business, be compassionate about the people, understand the financials of the organization, and understand the company's past and its drivers for the future – then put himself or herself in the same line as an executive partner of the company. CTOs should never be technology geeks. They should always be thinkers on behalf of the business, with a technology bias. If they represent themselves as a technology geek, they will never be allowed to have the gut check with the C level individuals; it's just not permitted. But if they are business partners, and they understand the working and value propositions of the business, then they will be invited to participate at the most senior levels.

The Golden Rules of the CTO

The first golden rule is to place personal interests aside as much as possible and make the decisions that tend to be the best for the company. Above all, you must try to remove yourself from the vision of how decisions will benefit you.

The second rule is to bring the integrity of your office to bear upon your resources, your network, and everything you stand for when you are ready to play.

The third golden rule is to be committed to helping the corporation evolve itself in the way the collective corporation sees fit, but with the caveat that honesty and fair play must always be present.

Finally, an element of giving back is one of the most important contributions we all make as leaders. The most successful CTOs contribute to the communities around them, the ones outside the business. Such contributions truly keep us in touch with the realities of life. When we take this particular step and make these types of commitments, CTOs truly demonstrate leadership for their companies and serve a larger purpose, as well – improving our society.

Changes in Technology in the Future

The biggest change we'll have to face in the future is the increasing focus on privacy and security. I think the second major focus will be on the pace at which business continues to change and the acceleration to find the new business value propositions. Third, we will tend to support more individual intrusion of technology. We will bring technology into our daily lives, and that intrusion will occur with increasing speed.

I think another impact that technology will have is that the ubiquitous nature of technology will continue to flourish, which will cause more stress and conflict between work and personal life. Most of us have no concept of what we're going to do with the speed at which we'll be able to find and do things. Our level of tolerance for things that aren't fast, accurate, and integrated is going to quickly diminish.

I think the next generation of individuals will come into the business world, look at what we've done, look at the current generation and say, "You've brought together the foundations of technology, but *we* actually understand how to use it and integrate it better in our lives than you did. After all, we've never known a world without Internet access. We're now going to change the directions of technology to be more reflective of new life-functioning ways."

This positioning by the next generation will become almost as unimaginable for us as we move into our elder days as our current technology revolution has been for our parents. The future we will receive from the next generation will bring with it all of the principles that we somehow created. Let's hope that we paid as much attention to thinking about people as CTOs as we paid to thinking about the technology.

Richard Schroth, as Perot Systems' chief technology officer, has added a strong focus on the market-facing elements of the company's technology efforts, further enabling Perot Systems to assess and lead our customers' visions of technology and business process, especially at strategic levels.

Dr. Schroth, who joined Perot Systems in 2001, is regarded as one of the most sought-after independent technology strategists, thought leaders, and international presenters on management issues and the application of emerging technologies. He has more than 23 years of experience directing strategic use of technology and is well known for his work in business strategy and emerging technology development. He has served as a trusted advisor to a wide range of top executives and companies throughout his career, both domestically and internationally.

Before founding Executive Insights, where he provided private advisory and speaking services, Dr. Schroth served as senior vice president of research and advisory services for Computer Sciences Corporation (CSC). There he co-founded Vanguard, one of the most successful, advanced technology advisory services in the world. While at CSC, he was also involved with four of the largest outsourcing engagements in the industry (General Dynamics, Hughes Electronics, British Aerospace, and J.P. Morgan). Before working at CSC, Dr. Schroth served as chief technology officer for Marriott Corporation, where he reported directly to Mr. Marriott.

Dr. Schroth has a doctorate from Indiana University, a master's degree from the University of Illinois, and a bachelor's degree from Western Illinois University. He has also served as a Senior Visiting Fellow at the Wharton School of Business and was a member of the Executive Education Faculty at AT&T for five years.

INNOVATION DRIVES BUSINESS SUCCESS

KIRILL TATARINOV

BMC Software

Senior Vice President,
Chief Technology Officer

The Role of the CTO

The role of the CTO means different things in different companies. I think when we describe the role, we must clearly distinguish and describe what we're talking about. The role of the CTO in a small startup company is often that of founder. That is not the role of CTO I am going to describe. There is also the CTO, typically in European and Israeli companies, who manages research and development. I will not describe this CTO's role, either. I'm going to talk about the role of the CTO in Fortune 500 high-tech companies, primarily in the United States.

The problem that large, publicly traded corporations have is that they are driven by quarterly earnings and by very strict measures. It's very hard for those organizations to innovate, and it's very difficult for those companies to make sure they are staying on the leading edge and aren't just sticking to current tactical deliverables. In these large corporations, the role of CTO is responsible for bringing in innovations, making sure the corporation pays attention to new technology, spending precious resources on delivering innovative ideas and new technologies, and promoting it both within the company and outside the company. It's also important to rally the technical engineering forces inside the company to be able to innovate.

There are multiple facets to innovation. Internal incubators are created in some companies to foster this idea development. The CTO might establish some additional incentives to promote the generation of ideas and applications for patents and things of that nature. Essentially, the key for the CTO in a large company is to push innovation and make sure the organization does not slide down into just delivering quarterly results.

The role of the CTO in a large, high-tech company is to make sure the organization is ready for the next major new technology cycle. Technology delivers a highly innovative and challenging environment with an incredible pace of change. It's very exciting to be a part of an industry that is constantly changing and progressing as we discover new ways to adapt technology for benefits in our everyday lives. As chief technologist, I am responsible for guiding the strategy for developing solutions that large companies use to keep their businesses up and running every day. This is both a great responsibility and a wonderful opportunity.

Defining Success

Success for the CTO does not really have a tangible measure. I think perception, communication, sharing of ideas, and creating the innovator's aura around the company are the main measures of the CTO. Very few companies in our industry and very few companies in the Fortune 500 ranks can brag about being innovators. The list of the top five software companies, for example, contains not one innovator primarily, I think, because CTOs are not present or not empowered or are just driven by more tactically oriented objectives. Success is the innovative aura a company has about itself.

High-tech companies all have research and development (R&D) driving them. The return on investment for research, however, is often not tangible. One measure of a CTO's success is benchmarking the return on R&D investments through proper prioritization of goals. To be successful, a business must generate profit, and R&D is the foundation for future company profits. No matter how good your product is, you will always need to continue enhancing it through research, or it will be left behind in the market as competitors build the proverbial "better mousetrap." As a member of the executive team, the CTO must help drive profitability to increase shareholder return.

Keeping up to Speed With Technology

I use a couple of techniques to stay current with technology and to make sure we have a chance to take advantage of the most appropriate trends. One is basically having information and knowledge readily available. It's important to find the right sources of information and keep yourself and your team knowledgeable to understand what's going on in the industry. This is not something one person can handle alone. The amount of information available right now is so huge that it's impossible to stay on top of everything. A successful CTO should have a CTO office filled with smart people devoted to different technology areas. For example, I have a person responsible for wireless, a person responsible for appliances, etc., and I have frequent focus group meetings with my team. I want very smart, highly educated people who are able to grasp, visualize, and conceptualize new technologies and present new ideas on how those technologies can be applied to the business of our company. It's a combination of continuous knowledge and staying abreast of developments in the marketplace. We must have knowledge of our own business and our own product to drive internal development. It takes a lot of sharing, communicating, intuitive thinking, and conceptualizing.

Choosing the Right Technologies

As the CTO, I am responsible for delivering the technology our customers require to maintain availability and performance for their Fortune 1000 companies. I am in charge of setting the vision and the strategy, as well as ensuring that we are delivering the solutions that our customers need, when they need them.

I'm a very pragmatic person. I try to be careful with "cool stuff." Cool stuff is great, but I leave my people in the CTO office to play with it. At the same time, I'm trying to make sure we keep this cool stuff from the developers who actually write production code. The cool stuff is dangerous. I believe the cool stuff is not fully proved, and it doesn't have the stamp of the industry on it. Again, much information is available on the adoption rate; you can gain many industry examples and a lot of industry knowledge by communicating with your peers and other companies. You can gain knowledge by communicating with the actual designer or inventor of this technology. In general, I would say I do not want BMC to be the first to use a certain technology in the industry – unless, of course, we created it. I want proof that this technology has worked for somebody else before I recommend applying it to one of BMC's products.

The reason for that is very simple. Typically, our product is the last line of defense in a large IT department. Our products make sure mission-critical applications are up and running at all times. If our product is built on some cool but unproven technology, and because of that, it fails, credit card companies stop processing cards; telephone companies stop processing calls; and the business starts to collapse. Obviously, that would be completely unacceptable.

New Technologies

I think wireless is extremely important. Wireless went through the cycle of euphoria, and now it's going down into a more pragmatic cycle. The rate of adoption by large enterprises is incredibly low. I think it will increase, and it's definitely a major trend that will drive the future. Coupled with wireless are personal communication devices that would essentially converge a wireless phone, an organizer, and e-mail devices into one. There's a long way to go for anyone to do that. Wireless communication is going to have to come up a notch. It has yet to be decided whether it's GPRS, what they call 2 ½ or 3G, or something else altogether, but the current wireless infrastructure will have to come up. I believe this is the most crucial element in today's technology – bringing wireless to the next level.

A lot of things are coming up right now in home automation, and very specific connective gadgets for the house and the office are being introduced. This is also a very intriguing area, but frankly, from just having attempted to automate my own house, I think that area needs a lot of work. There are no standards for home automation. There are no standards outside of the traditional PC. The whole push toward specialized gadgets and specialized devices that can be used for a lot of utilitarian purposes is going to be a major focus as we move forward.

BMC Software will soon roll out great new technology to address the needs of large enterprises to optimize their business through proactive management of the infrastructure and through integrated service management. The most important elements in this solution are the amount of intelligence and the predictive capabilities built into it. Companies today must do less with more. Even if resources aren't tight, it is sometimes impossible to hire the number of people you need to maintain a large enterprise.

Automation – solutions that are self-diagnostic and self-healing – helps administrators be more proactive, allowing them to do more with less. The large businesses of tomorrow will be more complex with interdependent systems. Our mission is to introduce technology to manage this complexity and to make it understandable and easy to implement for the business owner.

The Importance of Communication

If I were to summarize the role of the CTO in one word, it would be communicate. The most important role for the CTO is that of communicator. It's necessary to be able to identify key people in various organizations and communicate through those people or directly with engineers in those corporations to promote ideas and execute technology. That is the role of CTO – to communicate with those groups, promote common technology, promote technologies everyone will use, and work with general managers of those individual units to establish various incentives that will bring people to the new technology.

In traditional companies, R&D is primarily involved with designing products and creating prototypes to give to manufacturing to produce. In software, manufacturing does not exist, so R&D both builds and delivers the product to the market. This makes the line between research and development very blurry, sometimes making research disappear altogether due to the drive to develop product at the pace needed to fulfill customer demand. The challenge for the CTO is to make sure that research is present and empowered to move the company's strategic vision forward.

Privacy Issues

Privacy in general has been a concern to society for a long time – it is just getting a lot more attention lately. What the Internet has done, and what online collaboration and the Web have done, is magnify the existing problems ten-, hundred-, and thousand-fold. We had privacy issues before the Internet. We had credit card vendors selling our names and addresses. We had a lot of information about individuals being sold on paper. Now it can be done online. Now more information can be assembled about people online, on a much larger scale than ever before.

There will be a significant industry built to help people protect themselves. This industry exists today in the form of security and intrusion protection and intrusion prevention. Security software and the security industry will be big going forward. There will be a number of legislations that society will have to put in place, and I know our legislative board is very active in protecting consumers and protecting our privacy. A lot of software vendors will make sure they are protecting their customers. My team will also have the mandate to implement this legislation as it applies to our software solutions.

The next-generation computer system will need to have significant enhancements in security, so people can have things like firewalls in their machines straight out of the box, without having to acquire the software somewhere else. Just as you can lock the doors of your home and make your phone number unlisted, software of the future will give you similar protection from unwanted cyber-intrusions. Privacy is a big issue, but I think the industry and the government are dealing with it, and I think it will remain a top priority for quite some time.

The CTO as Part of the Executive Team

For a company to be innovative and have any chance to promote technology within the corporation, the CTO should be one of the top executives in the company. That is the case with BMC and most high-tech corporations. It is extremely important that the CTO interacts daily with the senior executive team and has a chance to participate in senior planning sessions to promote technology use through those meetings. The CTO and the CTO's team need to work very closely with the customer, promoting the company's innovative and technology-driven nature. That is an important part of the CTO's job. Technology use and promoting technology use by the corporation's outside customers, working in the field, and working with the sales organization to help them position the company in the high-tech competitive playing field are keys to a CTO's success.

Most importantly, if I identified new product opportunities and found new product areas for the use of new technology in the company, I would feel I am doing my job well. I would probably single that out as priority number one. There are many others. Frankly, in a high-tech corporation, very tactically on a day-to-day basis, the CTO is the most senior technical advisor to the CEO and president. That is my most important priority day-to-day. The CTO has to make sure the person who runs the company has enough knowledge and is making the right decisions related to technology and technology direction and innovation.

Taking Risks

In my opinion, large companies should not be taking significant technology risks in the mainstream areas of their business. This goes back to my earlier point of using only proven technologies when going to market. It's just not prudent, and it's irresponsible to do it any other way because the company needs to deliver value for the shareholders.

On the other hand, there are mechanisms and ways for large companies to take very significant risks without direct impact on the shareholders. For example, there is a whole area of corporate venturing where corporations like BMC will do minority investments in highly innovative, highly risky new ventures, dealing with completely unproven technologies. We're making these strategic bets in partnership with other large corporations and venture capitalists. We are watching the strategic bets in those new technologies. Once we see that those technologies can play a role in our future, and once we see the proof that those technologies can be applied to our mainstream business, we either license them or acquire them.

Most large corporations use a similar approach. In my mind we want a mechanism to balance the company's need for new technology and for funding new innovative ideas with shareholder value and not risking shareholder return, which is very important for any publicly traded Fortune 500 company.

Managing in Turbulent Times

I think you have to be more disciplined to manage in turbulent times than in a booming economy. To be successful, I think every manager has to go through a recession or an economic downturn like the one we've been experiencing. Or they have to go through the experience of downsizing in a corporation. It helps people build discipline. Discipline is what we need today. We need disciplined leaders who know how to manage the bottom line, make the right calls, set the right priorities, and make sure we're able to make money for the shareholders today, but at the same time not sacrifice our long-term future. Markets will come back up, and those who made the right calls will emerge as new leaders. It's all about discipline.

Each member of my team is expected to closely scrutinize every expense to ensure that we are getting the maximum ROI out of our limited resources. We are re-prioritizing products, while maintaining our focus on our customers' critical business needs. At the same time, I'm focused on fostering the innovative spirit both within my team and companywide as we look for ways to deliver more value with fewer resources. Especially important is keeping the lines of communication open with my team, so that we are a part of making decisions that will affect our jobs and the products that we support. This is the true measure of success when managing in turbulent times.

As in any other economic downturn, technology has helped businesses get out of the slump. For consumers to start buying again, there has to be innovative technology that gets everyone excited and eager to make purchases. I am thrilled to have the opportunity to participate in the high-tech revolution that will lead to economic recovery.

Best Business Advice

Know your field and know your technology. That is the most important advice I can give to a CTO. Once you become a business leader, you cannot lose sight of the importance of keeping up with technology.

Communication is another important skill to have and will take a CTO very far. Conceptualizing and summarizing ideas is valuable in the day-to-day life of the CTO. The amount of information out there right now is huge, and unless you can conceptualize the information, you will not be able to grasp the ideas necessary to do a good job. The CTO has to be able to grasp these ideas and communicate them companywide.

Understanding the engineers and continuing to be an engineer while you are an executive is also very important.

Becoming a Technology Leader

It takes a number of qualities to make an exceptional leader. A great leader needs to have outstanding people skills and be able to relate to everyone from the executives to the newest and most junior members of the team. The ability to both create and clearly articulate a strategy and a vision is also an important skill. A good leader then needs to be able to communicate this vision to large groups of people to make them both believers in and followers of the vision, while giving them room to contribute their talents and ideas. In IT, it's also important to have a deep understanding of the technology details, and yet, to be able to move quickly to the highest level of abstraction.

Leadership in technology takes very strong technical knowledge of the field of the business of the company. I think it also takes very strong knowledge of the environment the company is experiencing to make good decisions. The technology ideas have to be applied to the business to be successful. It takes strong communication skills. Being a CTO is all about communicating with others and particularly with engineers. Being able to speak with engineers in their language is important. Engineers speak a different language and have a different way of thinking than the usual business crowd. In many companies, the CTO plays the role of interpreter between the business leader and the engineers. This is a very important role because it is critical for the business team to understand the role of the engineers, while giving the engineers insight into what they need to deliver to attain the company's overall business goals.

Staying current with the latest technical advances in your company's business is another important issue. Continuously communicate with the senior management of the company. Stay close to the engineers and engineering management in the company. Most importantly, don't lose touch with your customers in the marketplace.

The hardest part of my job as CTO is persuading large groups of people to follow technology directions without having any direct authority over these people. A typical organization's business units and actual production units do not report to the CTO. CTOs often do not have authority over the people who have to implement their strategic directions. Being able to influence the business units and articulate where technologies and the engineers need to go, without having direct authority, has its challenges. Yet again, it requires a great deal of communication and interpersonal skills.

Keeping Your Edge

What helps me most in keeping my edge is surrounding myself with smart people who deal with multiple technology areas over time and interacting with those people daily. A good CTO cannot lead by hiding behind the office as the "supreme ruler." It is important to regularly meet with your team and to visit with members of your team on all levels. This will give you a much clearer picture of the true state of your organization. Nothing replaces direct interaction. Talking to people on a continual basis, both inside and outside the company, who are directly involved in innovating new technologies is very important. And, of course, reading industry publications and visiting industry Web sites help a CTO remain knowledgeable.

As far as publications are concerned, it's very important to identify sources of information that are available by subscription. You can receive a one-page e-mail in your inbox every morning that keeps you abreast of the latest trends and news relevant to your job. Today most of the magazines have a service like that. Some publications actually have specialized focused mailings going directly to CTOs, so you get highly summarized pockets of information. If you find it interesting, you can follow the link and find more information and spend more time reading. This kind of information is invaluable and well worth the time it takes to read it.

My Dream Technology

To be able to get to any place without lengthy travel would be my dream. It's very important to me personally because I've lived in many countries around the world. My family – my parents and my sister – live in Australia, and I have friends all over Europe.

I just wish that in my lifetime the day would come when I could tele-transport myself to Australia for dinner this evening, spend the night with my parents, and be back in my office the next morning.

The Golden Rules of Technology

Rule number one: No technology for the sake of technology. Focus on customer benefits. Too many times we've seen someone get carried away by technology and start building something without a clear purpose or goals. As I mentioned, it is the CTO's job to drive value for the business through technology innovation. Technology innovation creates the products that the customers need and will purchase, and technology innovation will drive increasing revenues.

Rule number two: Technology is for the bigger context, for your corporation and for humanity at large. Any new technology is part of the evolution of society. It needs to be built with that thought in mind. Technology should be made available to the community at large through patents and other means. Although it is necessary to maintain your company's competitive advantage, it is important to contribute to projects that promote the greater good of society as a whole.

The Future of Technology

The next economic boom will be driven by the latest advancements in technology. I think that is paramount. We have to create new ideas that will drive consumption again.

I think we're going to see wireless come to the next level. I think we'll see automation of lifecycles come to different levels. We'll see voice recognition come to a higher level. We'll see visualization and user interface come to a significantly more intuitive level. Holographic three-dimensional images will replace today's flat screens and boring presentations.

The computing power is there. It's just a matter of building applications. I'm really looking forward to the next ten years. I think right now we're at a stage where we're going to come to the next quantum leap when technology advances. We've been living in the era of PCs for the last ten years, and we're about to begin something innovative and exciting.

Kirill Tatarinov is senior vice president and chief technology officer for BMC Software, Inc. In this role, he is focused on driving the company's technical vision and strategy, including common technology platforms. He is also responsible for four of the company's business units, including Network and Enterprise E-business Management.

Before taking this position, Mr. Tatarinov was the vice president of corporate development for BMC Software, where he was responsible for merger and acquisition, strategic planning, and advanced research activities. Tatarinov was also responsible for Patrol business for BMC Software from 1994 until 1997.

Mr. Tatarinov joined BMC Software in January 1994 with the acquisition of Patrol Software, Pty. Ltd., where he served as head of research and development, chief architect, and co-founder. Mr. Tatarinov has more than 15 years of experience in the architecture, development, and management of enterprise software. Before co-founding Patrol Software in 1991, he was with several computer and networking companies.

Mr. Tatarinov holds a master's degree in computers from the Moscow University for Transport Engineering (MIIT) and an MBA from the Houston Baptist University.

MANAGING THE TECHNOLOGY KNOWLEDGE

DR. SCOTT DIETZEN

BEA E-Commerce Server Division

Chief Technology Officer

The Role of the CTO

My role as chief technology officer is very inter-disciplinary. Working internally, I'm expected to provide high-level direction, as well as be a cheerleader and coach for the engineering organization. I look after key initiatives and help mold the product from the big-picture perspective. On occasion, the CTO needs to ensure the organization doesn't "lose site of the forest for the trees." All this requires very close collaboration with engineering, product management, and product marketing to represent marketplace requirements and ensure our products best meet those requirements.

While internal responsibilities are a big part of my job, I have as many or more external responsibilities. I spend at least half my time with our large customers, our independent software vendors (ISVs), our systems integrators, industry analysts, and financial analysts. All these people have a vested interest in understanding our business and technology direction.

One of the things I find most compelling about my role as CTO is that it lets me mix technology and business. Somewhere along the line, in my education, I decided that technology for technology's sake wasn't nearly as interesting as technology that could transform the way people live and work. Which is why I work so hard to help transfer BEA's technology into the marketplace.

Most of all, the CTO role demands that I fit well within the greater BEA team. In essence, the CTO job is to project the overall technology direction and vision for BEA. That's a job far too big for any individual.

The Impact of the CTO

The single most gratifying thing about being a CTO is to have your technology ideas broadly used and adopted. High-tech CTOs measure their success by the success of the technology their companies bring to market. However, as I said before, it is very much a team effort all of the time. A CTO is often expected to be the best architect, the best engineer, and sometimes even the best business strategist for his or her company. I can tell you I fail on all accounts at BEA. Instead, I get to play the "lead singer," if you will, for a large and extremely gifted "rock band." At some level, I'm expected to take credit for the great work that gets done all across the organization, and I do my best to make sure I relay that credit back to the ones who really deserve it. That's number one. Taking responsibility for problems is number two. Pass the credit, but take the blame is the credo for any leader, including a CTO.

The other obviously great thing about being a CTO is getting to interact with so many gifted people, both inside and outside the company: I get to meet with the best minds of our business partners and customers, as well as BEA's own superstars. So I'm constantly exchanging ideas with a lot of really smart people. I can't help becoming more educated myself as a result of that exposure.

I'm often asked, "How can you manage to keep up with all the latest technology initiatives?" It actually happens naturally because of all the help I'm getting. I'm constantly interacting with bright people trying to solve business problems with technology – smart people from little startup companies to ones within global 2000 end-users. So I'm getting to see these new ideas early on, and then I start forming conclusions about how they're going to make an impact on the broader industry down the road. And when I do make a mistake, our competitors will ensure that we get it right by making the case directly to the market.

Keeping Your Edge

Keeping my edge really does come down to my commitment and my network. You have to work hard and read voraciously, but far more valuable to me is the network I cultivate.

I maintain an internal network of the most gifted people at BEA – they're not only my colleagues, but generally my friends, as well. I also have a broad network outside of BEA, so I'm often engaged in talking to technology leaders in many different businesses. When they encounter something they think is interesting or compelling, I'll get a heads-up. When things happen, I typically don't need to go out and shake the trees; I'm lucky enough that my network will alert me.

Another important point is not to mistake organizational charts for a network – a CTO must cultivate the technology leaders independent of how they report into management.

Those networks are absolutely essential to CTOs. You have to have them internally because that's how you influence and direct the engineering organization. They're probably even more important externally. CTOs who get too internally focused lose touch with the marketplace, and as a result, end up making mistakes. So part of the CTO's job is to keep the company grounded – that is, in touch with what's going on in the marketplace, so the right things are happening inside the company to exploit the ever changing opportunities.

Near-term Projecting and Planning

I don't think there's any magic to making projections and plans. It requires a lot of communication with your customers and business partners. Your customers tell you what their IT challenges are, and your business partners roll up their own collected information on the challenges their customers are facing. You mix that in with the new technology direction and look at the broad initiatives that are under way – the standard technologies and the startup companies.

One of the biggest challenges is trying to find the pearls. The vast, vast majority of new technology initiatives flounder, just like new startups. You really have to be able to see through the marketing hype associated with early-stage technologies to avoid dead ends and technologies that aren't yet mature.

For example, BEA did some early investigation into WAP technology – the Wireless Application Protocol – which sounded very appealing at the time. But we had some reservations about how quickly the infrastructure could be built out. Moreover, we were concerned about not yet having always-on connectivity to the mobile device (i.e., packet switching networks), and that very early on WAP was positioned as an Internet competitor. As a result, we actually did not make a big investment in WAP technology ourselves; instead, we took a wait-and-see approach while we worked closely with our strategic partners. And as it has turned out, that was the right thing to do. Today, we have numerous WAP deployments around the world, but we didn't invest our own engineering dollars in building specific technologies that are being superseded over time.

So as I'm constantly looking at new technologies, I tend to classify them as buy, sell, hold, and undetermined. "Buys" are technologies such as Java, Web services, and XML, which we believe will have or are already having a very substantial impact on the market. "Sell" technologies tend to be more legacy technologies, and we at BEA don't really have very much of that. There are a couple of more mature products, one called Object Broker and a transaction processing technology called Top End, which we're no longer investing big dollars in. Those technologies still support our customers' needs, but they don't justify a substantial investment going forward. "Hold" technologies are those that may no longer be growing fast, but we still have to look after the investment and make sure they remain viable. "Undetermined" is the whole fringe of new technologies that we're always looking at and trying to determine where they fit into the puzzle.

You make some mistakes – I'm sure I make at least one every day. But the key is not to get paralyzed. People have a natural decision-making process, and I've learned to respect my own. I dabble with the technology, mostly by reading specifications and conversing with my peers, until I get an intuition about what's going to happen with it, as opposed to forcing myself to make a decision too early. On the other hand, you must be careful not to flounder because there's just way, way too much going on in the marketplace.

The single biggest challenge for CTOs is the same as for other executives: How do I slice my time thinly enough that I get done all the things I need to get done and still have a substantive impact where I need to have one?

The Future of Web Services

There have been several candidates for establishing a universal grid, or backbone, if you will, through which to interconnect all applications. The Common Object Request Broker Architecture (CORBA) was one such proposed solution. Next, many envisioned that Java would become ubiquitous on both clients and servers, and hence that the future of integration would become passing Java objects back and forth across the network (Java becomes the lingua franca of the integration). Certainly, those visions have failed to materialize so far.

Web services is the next candidate, and one I'm very bullish on. The World-Wide Web has already universally connected our clients to both applications and documents, everywhere around the world, with nearly instantaneous access. Because that infrastructure is already in place, it now seems very natural and compelling to leverage that fabric, with some slight extensions, for application-to-application communications. For integration, we need to replace HTML with XML, and there are some additional technologies, such as reliable asynchronous messaging and security technologies that we need above the basic Web protocols to make all of this work. However, the best news about Web services is that (1) the majority of the stack has been being hardened for years; (2) it's far easier than its forerunners; and (3) it presumes much less knowledge about the service consumer. I would characterize the last one as loose-coupling, and it's fundamental to trying to address integration at the scale of the Web.

That is the promise of Web services. I think the value proposition is indeed compelling because BEA's largest customers have tens of thousands of applications, and right now, those applications talk to only their closest related siblings, often within silos. Each of our customers' businesses is becoming more specialized every day, and that specialization means they need not just their own sophisticated business applications – some of them built in-house, most of them bought outside – but it also means they need to divest themselves of things they don't do quite as well. That means they're becoming more interconnected with their business partners, as well as more interconnected internally.

So, clearly, I see the demand for communications between applications being driven up dramatically, and there's only one way we can be successful. We can't afford to do these integrations point-to-point or few-to-few, which is what the historical approach was: Application A talks to Application B. Instead, you set up both Application A and Application B to talk to the same backbone, so they can work together.

Most of all, this backbone cannot be proprietary. Without the standards of HTML, HTTP, and SSL, we would have no World Wide Web. Web services have emerged as the Web solution for the business imperative of integration.

This build-out will be significant over the next few years. Enterprises will first build out internally, and then go external. We're seeing more demand for enterprise application integration than we are for B2B (Business-to-Business) right now. That's a fine way for these technologies to be proved out.

The Future of Wireless

Wireless solutions remain very popular, although adoption is uneven. We see the most traction in the carrier and enterprise (mobile intranet) marketplaces. By the way, we've stopped using the term "wireless" directly inside BEA; we actually talk about "pervasive computing" and the continuing specialization of devices to better meet user demands, and we talk about "multi-channel" to mean the integrated combination of Web, wireless Web, text and instant messaging, voice, and programmed clients (such as Java, C, or Visual Basic client applications).

Everybody talks about devices consolidating, such as phone and PDA, but I tend to think that's not going to happen. We've recently seen the emergence of blackberries, or "crackberries," as they're known by their addicts. I just see much more proliferation because people have many different usage models around technology. Rather than single comprehensive devices, I think there'll be lots of little devices. The mobile work force may use a device different from a telephone or a generic PDA. And I think this proliferation is good. Of course, these devices are not just for people. We can interconnect many other devices, such as on-board navigation systems, so we can get real-time traffic conditions or an open gas station. In San Francisco, my idea of a killer app is a satellite that can find you the closest parking space.

All of these information devices need to get connected, and one critical piece of that effort will be Web services. For application programs that are running on such devices, Web services is the most natural model for how an application communicates, checks, and updates itself with the rest of the world. So Web services isn't just about server-to-server communication; it can also be about client-to-server communication.

The Future of Java

There are a number of very broad initiatives around Java. If you look at the platform, there's a Java implementation targeted for the PC and general client environment; an implementation that's targeted for the mobile pervasive computing environment; and a Java platform targeted for server infrastructure.

At BEA, we remain the most bullish about server-side Java. In fact, we've built much of our business around making server-side Java and Java 2 Enterprise Edition (J2EE) the raging success that it is. Early on, the rest of the market for Java was very excited about the next-generation client, and all the press was about Java challenging Windows on the desktop. From BEA's perspective, we believed if Java was going to be a success for the client, hallelujah, but much more importantly, this sure looks like a great language for automating business processes on the server!

Moreover, if the Web is going to take off, the Web has to be thin-client. It can't be a thick PC client model because a Charles Schwab can never put their trading logic into an applet and download it to the client machine because then their competitors would have access to it. How would you secure it? How would you manage it? How would you protect your corporate data against tampering? Thick-client doesn't fit on the Web, which is why Microsoft has evolved their strategy so dramatically to accommodate the Web paradigm.

We're now branching out by not just attracting applications, but integration challenges, as well. We've been talking about Web services as a platform for integration. But now the underlying Java J2EE standard has itself been extended for integration. So in addition to hosting new applications, we see a really broad business perpetuating our WebLogic Java platform to help address many of the integration challenges facing enterprises. Some of these enterprises will use

WebLogic directly. Others will adopt WebLogic embedded within the value-added offerings of our integration-focused partners.

A couple of very large independent software vendors are touting to the market that integration is too hard – that your only solution is to buy all your applications from a single supplier. Even if such a single-vendor application family is not as good from a business perspective, at least they're pre-integrated (despite that they're not really integrated). I would call that approach "worst of breed" and find it very distasteful.

The industry has to step up to reduce the pain associated with "best of breed" for the connected world. Best of breed was fine while applications didn't have to intercommunicate. Now that they do, we have to bring down the hurdles between them. Web services is a key technology for doing that, but Java is also compelling because there are now Java standard adaptors for connecting in legacy systems. Java provides a very rich framework for processing XML and Web services.

Privacy, Security, and Trust Issues

My e-mail address is exposed to the world, and as you would expect, I'm now inundated with garbage. I haven't been the victim of identity theft yet, knock on wood, but I haven't figured out how to deal with being overwhelmed with information and requests. Having a great executive administrator is critical.

Plenty of people are still uncomfortable about leveraging online technology because of security, and many more businesses are trying to understand their own exposure and that of their business partners. The key for us, as one of the technology infrastructure providers, is to ensure there are no security holes within our platform that might open up a back door to hackers. However, the onus is still on the end-user to ensure their specific technology deployments are appropriately hardened.

I'm also quite excited about the new technologies – the Microsoft initiatives around Passport and Hailstorm – and AOL has an initiative (widely reported in the press) called Magic Carpet. Yahoo! may also be weighing in. These initiatives will help users because they need not enter the same information over and over again across different Web sites. Instead, we input information once and then grant rights to it as we see fit. But it doesn't change the fact that the organizations we're doing business with are still able to abuse it, once we give it to them. The only solution to the latter problem is simply not to grant information to organizations you don't trust. Perhaps legislation will sometime set up appropriate boundaries as to how the information we grant is used and abused. Until then, we're all stuck either reading the fine print on the privacy agreements on the Web site (and believing it), or assuming the worst and holding back the information.

There's also a question of knowing what the right legislation is. I tend not to enter my credit card information on the Web to Joe Bob's Book Shop because I don't have a relationship with them. But I do have a relationship with Amazon, from which I order probably two or three things a week. In four years of doing business with them, as far as I can tell, they've never abused my relationship with them. So for now, I'd say "buyer beware" seems to be working reasonably well and does not appear to be holding back growth of the Web.

By the way, I expect much the same kind of growth for B2B on top of the Web services platform. B2B similarly depends upon trust relationships. We simply aren't going to empower our business application to pick our business partners any time soon. Amazon doesn't want to discover their next year of shipping contracts will be serviced by Jim Bob's Delivery. Instead, they cultivate business relationships with trusted business partners. In other words, for the foreseeable future, dynamic discovery of services will be much more interesting on intranets and among trusted trading partners than it will be on the Internet.

Keeping BEA Flexible and On-Target

I'll occasionally go to our engineers and complain that this or that issue seems to have fallen off the roadmap. We have to get it back on track, either because our customers will demand it, or it'll give us some compelling advantage against our competitors. Then our engineers will come back to me and say, "Well, you have to give up something in return. What'll it be?" And together with engineering and product management, we'll have to make the trade-off.

To ensure this flexibility, we work pretty hard to keep our engineering assignments fluid. We want our engineers to be generalists first – we want to give them a chance to work on a lot of different areas of our products. We'll actually move engineering tasks from place to place, lab to lab, and switch people on and off. We have a very rich community infrastructure that allows us to do distributed development, across time zones and geographies, and allows us to do this re-purposing of engineers on various projects without sacrificing the coherence and tight integration that our customers expect.

Distributed development is one of BEA's special secret sauces that we've been honing over the years. It doesn't seem to happen too much in the industry – generally, where distributed development is done, the resulting products are not tightly integrated the way we think successful products have to be. We work very hard to be good at that.

In terms of keeping up with new technologies, the engineering organization itself – an extremely gifted, motivated team – will come up with many more great ideas than I or my team ever could. I'm consistently happily surprised at the functionality that comes together, much of which I learn about after the product goes into beta!

For this most recent JavaOne (our most important show), we gave a really compelling demo of our Web services technology, showing how we made Web services transparent for the Java programmer. The truth is XML can be awfully tedious for any programmer, and to make that work so easily seems like magic. I'd love to say it was my idea to develop this compelling demonstration that showed how to consume Web services and even generate new Web services by writing a couple of lines of Java code, and that I then went to engineering and said this is what we ought to do. But, in fact, I just talked about the need for Web services, and this stellar team came up with this on their own. That's why "A" players in engineering and product management are the biggest boon to a CTO. I often have the luxury of simply rationalizing their contributions in retrospect, rather than identifying a hole in our strategy.

Their reward is that we shower praise on them. In fact, one of the engineers behind that initiative just got a quarterly award and a lot of visibility. This is a key part of what the CTO needs to do: draw recognition and reward to exactly those kinds of entrepreneurial initiatives.

The number-one requirement for a CTO is fostering talent within the organization. I submit that a small team of "A" players is a necessary (but not sufficient) condition for the launch of any successful product. Also, while I know this is trite, only an "A" team can hire other "A" players. "B" teams hire "C" players. And "C" teams can't hire anybody. It's all about keeping a critical mass of superstar talent and making sure they are all given the room to do what they do well, and that they are justly rewarded. That is something the whole organization has to sign up for.

Managing and Selecting Risks

I think the key for information technology is that a very small number of people can have a huge impact. Software is a purely intellectual product, which, like music or art, dramatically amplifies the contribution that gifted individuals can make. So while on a construction line, you'd be amazed to hear one worker is twice as productive as another, in software you can see productivity differences of ten- and even twenty-fold.

Of course, the reality for software is also that a substantial maintenance cost is associated with it. We have 11,000 customers, and some of those customers have 100 or 200 applications. Keeping that community happy is hard work. So there is an inherent, built-in cost to software products that you have to account for. The risk is understaffing, which will quickly alienate customers. It helps to have objective measures of customer satisfaction, so you can avoid such pitfalls.

The greatest risk to a CTO generally comes from new, displacing technologies. In my mind, managing risk means not over-committing to new initiatives. I think one of the biggest mistakes businesses make is deciding some initiative is strategic and then putting 20 or 30 software engineers on it. Starting from scratch like that is crazy. It's so much less effective than putting three or four hotshots on it for the first six months, which you probably should have done six to nine months ago, before you now think you need to put 30 on it.

That's something we have done supremely well – recognizing some of the key new trends early. We started investing in Java in 1995 and in Web services more than two years ago. So we're in a great position. We're always looking at what we think the key winning technologies will be, so we can be on that leading adoption curve. You just need to place the right bets, since few businesses can afford to cover all new technologies.

Managing in a Turbulent Market

There are some striking differences in managing in up-cycle and down-cycle markets. I liken the current market conditions to a hangover after a big party. Everybody's just looking around at the house and saying, "Wow, this place is trashed. I gotta clean it up." We're just not ready to open the doors and do some partying again till we work through some of this mess we've inherited.

I was on Wall Street recently, and some very large banks and investment brokerages were all talking about cost-reduction initiatives. Information technology budgets were being assigned around clean-up, rather than going out and attacking new markets and bringing in new revenues. I found that compelling. It says at some level that whatever Mr. Greenspan (Federal Reserve Chairman Alan Greenspan) does in the short term isn't necessarily going to jump-start a market that is inwardly-focused, trying to clean up the mistakes that resulted from trying to keep up with the explosive growth of the past few years.

For platform companies like ours, it means we need to focus on proving out our technologies' return on investment. While the market was growing explosively, people had an easier time of justifying purchases of Web application servers, since they were essential for e-business. Now, the users are more carefully qualifying purchases, since not every e-business application is a winning application. Of course, information technology is as much about saving money as finding new markets. We're working on applications now that will save tens of millions of dollars for our large customers, but it does change the way you approach the marketplace.

I think, internally, you have to be very focused on managing the bottom line. BEA is a public company, and it has always had those challenges and expectations around our level of profitability and expected achievement. So we've always been very careful to manage cost-effectively.

What that means to me, in the hyper-competitive business we're in, is we have to manage out our bottom performers. In a more conservative marketplace like today's, we're able to attract supremely gifted people. Maybe they were in a small startup or a dot-com, and now they are looking for something a little more stable. Maybe they were one of our competitors that fell by the wayside, and they want to get with a winner. In a down market, the leaders have the opportunity to upgrade some under-performers. This may not sound nice, but it's absolutely essential for the strength of the overall team. Indeed, the silver lining of the down market is to weed out the competitors.

All the statistics show that even though our own growth rate may be less than it was, we're still growing faster than the market, meaning we're taking market share from our competitors – a very large market, long-term. If you're managing for the long term, I think the important thing is cost control and making sure you're properly positioning your technology to solve the business problems your customers are facing today.

Becoming a Technology Leader

To become a technology leader, you have to be smart. You have to have the capacity to assimilate technology. I think you also have to be charismatic and gregarious – people need to like you and want to talk to you. You have to have good people skills because your job is to facilitate communication. Broadly, you're taking the summation of the engineering organization and the summation of the customer-partner-analyst input, and you're mapping information back and forth between the two.

You have to have a lot of bandwidth to be a CTO. A lot of supremely gifted engineers – plenty of them who are way smarter than I am – are not comfortable getting hundreds of e-mails a day and trying to have a broad but shallow impact on so many different initiatives. Instead, they'd much rather go deep on one or a smaller number of specific issues. This choice follows personality inclination.

CTOs also occasionally have to be able to get in deep, quickly, so I think another key trait is being intuitive in terms of looking at some technology for a short time and being able to size up its impact from incomplete information. You have to be able to come to opinions quickly, knowing that some of them will have to be revised later.

Then, I think there's a natural part of leadership that comes out of personal integrity. You have to be seen not just talking the talk, but walking the walk.

And you have to be able to demonstrate your product, get in there and get your hands dirty. That gives you a lot of additional credibility across the whole marketplace.

Finally, a CTO has to understand the business side. When I meet with a software vendor, I have to be able to look at what they do and understand not only the technical relationship between what they do and what BEA does, but also what the right business model is for partnership. It's actually not possible for the business guys alone, who don't understand the technology, to sort that out. So you often have to give them the business directives, as well. The CTO position really targets natural leaders who are technology-focused and gregarious, who want to keep one foot in the technology world and the other in the business world, and who want to build up their frequent flier miles.

Changes in Technology Going Forward

For sure, the broadest technology trend will continue – technology will continue to have more and more of an impact on our lives and our businesses. CTOs can't be luddites; it's incompatible with the job. Of course, the Internet has had a dramatic impact on business: Look at the Web and what information and services you have access to, sitting in your office or your home. The Web build-out has depended on a lot of server-side infrastructure in addition to the deployment of the Web browser. This second phase of the infrastructure build-out will leverage that infrastructure to deliver large-scale integration via Web services. We'll see the same network effect for Web-based integration that we saw for Web browsing.

There are still a lot of challenges ahead. One truly critical challenge for CTOs is how to deal with being inundated in general, and with e-mail specifically. At some level I feel like I'm a PERL script – I just sit there and route e-mails from one place to another, where I can hope they will have an impact. We have to get technology that will help us CTOs deal with all this noise.

But I couldn't be more excited to be part of the next five to ten years in terms of all this universal connectivity – not just among wire-line and wireless devices, but all the embedded devices from set-top boxes to automobile navigation systems to coffee makers, and that's going to bring in the nature of "killer" apps. Being one of the vendors that help deliver the overall infrastructure that helps make this vision possible is going to be a ton of fun.

Best Advice

The two best pieces of advice I ever received in business are (1) "Take ownership of your customer's success" and (2) "Time kills deals." The latter came from my mentor at the first startup I was part of, while the former is probably from my dad. If your customers are having a problem with your technology, that's wholly unacceptable. It's kind of ironic, but if a customer encounters a problem and gets a fix within a matter of hours, they'll actually think more of you than they did before they encountered the problem! Instill that kind of service ethic, that commitment to customer success, across your organization.

Second, complacency must be your competitor's problem. Business opportunities arise in a specific time and place. You need to be very aggressive in your attention to the priorities to close the critical win-win deals, although recognizing which ones are essential may not be obvious. If you encounter a deal that's a win for you, but not for your customer or partner, turn it into a win-win.

Golden Rules for CTOs

"Only the paranoid survive" remains a guiding principle. If you're doing something interesting, you're going to have a bunch of competitors. Competition is almost essential: Nothing creates market growth like vigorous competition. Of course, you need to compete fairly and with integrity. I value very much my integrity and the integrity with which BEA does business. Violating that integrity is not good business, even in the short term, let alone the long term. At the end of the day, if you're delivering compelling value to the customer, the market is going to take care of you.

Here's another way to think about it: When I was in college, many of us worked very hard to get good grades. But at some point, I decided I was just going to work hard at learning and let the grades look out for themselves. I found that liberating. Now I try to approach my job that same way. I find when I look at a customer's problem, a BEA product may not be the best fit. I'll ask if they've considered another product. Companies shouldn't push products that aren't the best fit for their customers; you only end up paying for it later. But no doubt the customer is going to look at you first next time.

So I think the key ingredients in the golden rules for CTOs are integrity, bandwidth, and energy – you have to be voracious in your appetite for keeping up with what's going on in the industry, talking and e-mailing to everyone. It's a very consuming role.

Fantasy Apps

If I could create any technology I could think of, I'd want to create something that would empower the uneducated music lover (such as myself), who doesn't know anything about constructing music, to become composers and orchestrators. There are a lot of people working on this, but I think it would be really neat to reduce the barriers to becoming more musically proficient. People who have already developed their listening skills find that these listening skills are so far ahead of their playing skills that it's really painful to try to play a piano or guitar. It's a daunting, many-year investment before they can enjoy listening to themselves.

Scott Dietzen is chief technology officer for the BEA E-Commerce Server Division. As chief technology officer, Dr. Dietzen is the technical strategist for all BEA E-Commerce Server products, including the award-winning BEA WebLogic Server, BEA WebLogic Enterprise and flagship, BEA Tuxedo. He also drives relationships with BEA's high-level partners, OEMs, and blue-chip customers. Dr. Dietzen is BEA's lead spokesperson on Java and the company's wireless development efforts. Before assuming his current role, Dr. Dietzen held the position of CTO for the BEA WebXpress Division.

Dr. Dietzen has more than ten years of experience with enterprise information systems, distributed application architectures, and business-critical deployments. He has spoken at numerous industry events and analyst conferences.

Before BEA's acquisition of WebLogic, Dietzen was WebLogic's vice president of marketing and product management and the lead business and technology spokesperson for the company. Before joining WebLogic, Dr. Dietzen was the principal technologist of Transarc Corporation, a developer of distributed systems for application deployment and global file-sharing. At Transarc, Dr. Dietzen drove the technical marketing strategy of Transarc's flagship product and co-founded and co-managed the enterprise sales channel, which accounted for most of Transarc's value when the business was sold to IBM in 1995.

Dr. Dietzen holds Ph.D. and Master of Science degrees in computer science and a Bachelor of Science degree in applied mathematics from Carnegie Mellon University.

THE CTO AS AN AGENT OF CHANGE

DOUG CAVIT

McAfee.com

Chief Technology Officer

The Emerging CTO

The world of information technology, especially in a new age of smarter infrastructure, is a continuously changing panorama that requires constant attention and adjustment. The most successful IT organizations are those that embrace the concept of continuous evolution. "Good enough" is never good enough. An organization that is not examining all levels of its IT vision, plans, infrastructure, and metrics is doomed to be less efficient and potentially outsourced.

The Internet revolution has fundamentally altered the existing relationship of information technology to the rest of the modern business organization. No longer is IT considered a tool to accomplish a particular purpose. IT and the technologies it delivers are now central to the ability of many enterprises to compete and harness the assets of knowledge workers worldwide.

Emerging from this major shift in the business world is the CTO. The CTO, in many instances the former CIO, is now an integral part of the business in his ability to track new trends, marry infrastructure with requirements, and build strategic partnerships that leverage any modern business. Aligning different business initiatives around the technology, whether in-house or outsourced, is a key part of what the CTO must deliver on a daily basis. All new technology ventures will be based on partnerships, in whole or in part. There are too many moving parts and too much cost efficiency not to embrace partnerships as an integral way of doing business. All of this is orchestrated by an individual who is not only technical but also business-literate. He or she must forge partnerships both internally and externally through good leadership and negotiation skills.

New Technologies, New Opportunities

During the past 30 years, we have seen the Internet change from a basic set of transport protocols to an expansive application platform that supports complicated transactions and large-scale data transport. But during the past two years, we have seen the rise of a completely new type of Internet service. This is the concept of the "Web service." Unlike the current Web browser and hyper-text markup languages

(HTML) platforms of the late 1990s or even the older paradigm of client/server computing, a Web service is a structured set of data that can be discovered, authenticated, and used without any particular client interface and without direct human interaction. This is at the center of what we provide and is quickly becoming the norm for many companies.

A Web service takes an inefficient form of electronic data transport and transforms it into something more efficient, reliable, and flexible. The heart of this new service is the use eXtensible Markup Language (XML). We use applications that employ XML to send "intelligent information" – not just data, but also the structure of the data – over the Internet, where it can then be used by intelligent agent applications on our customers' computers. XML has been extended to allow for automated discovery of services and for rich transports that can not only deliver data, but also recognize how best to interact with the information.

Web services alone are not as significant as the adoption of a common extensible platform that allows for universal collaboration among various Web services. This allows us to use services that are modular and can be combined to deliver complex applications. An example of this might be Web services that deliver authentication, e-mail, calendaring, and directory information. These can be combined to provide a complex application that allows people across organizations to schedule a meeting with a prospective client by automatically checking for calendar availability.

By adhering to standards, these services can come from any vendor, in any location, and on any type of computer platform. Web services also allow us to tap into the latent computer resources that we have on our client computers that are currently under-used. Complex operations, such as spreadsheet functions, could be performed on the client after the data was delivered via an XML Web service.

Web services represent a new challenge for the chief technology officer (CTO) on several fronts, beyond the usual issues of new and rapidly changing technologies. Web services force us to understand our customers in a much more detailed light. They compel us to consider infrastructure as a core competency, since these services depend on highly reliable Internet mechanisms. We will explore all of these concepts in more detail in this chapter.

Understanding the Customer

In many ways vendors focused on building Internet technologies have been more concerned with the best way to connect with one another, rather than with the customer. Last-mile connectivity and the "end user" experience were issues left to be sorted out by several vendors providing dial-up and telecom-based connectivity. As a result, we have come to expect slow and often unreliable access to the Internet and the services it provides.

If the Internet is to reach its full promise, we need to shift the focus away from internal connectivity issues and onto the end user. This is especially true with the advent of Web services, where the end user experience is completely determined by the type and quality of the end user's Internet connection. This dictates a "dial tone" level of availability and reliability, plus an ability to meet peak demands, placing every user on a level playing field for the quality of services provided. The content provider of tomorrow needs to focus on the end user experience and be engaged in every level of the infrastructure to ensure a high-quality user experience. As the Web becomes more personal, so does our focus on how to deliver the Web experience.

Infrastructure as a Competitive Advantage

Given the importance of the end-user experience, no longer is it adequate to have data leave a provider's location without thought about how it is to be received and used. We have to raise the importance of infrastructure to a new level. Infrastructure, which I define as our ability to deliver content to our end users, can become an increasingly forceful competitive tool as we strive to move into the new world of Web services. Companies that don't pay attention to the end-user experience, and especially the scalability and reliability of their infrastructure, run the risk of having their inattention used against them by their competitors in a business world where several different competing Web services exist.

For mission-critical software, such as security services or supply-chain management, the ability to reliably distribute information or services in a timely fashion can define a competitive advantage for a company. As Web services and other types of Internet services become an increasingly important part of our lives, the end user will naturally migrate to those services that are the most efficient and reliable. Businesses will promote their ability to deliver Web services as a means to differentiate their companies in a tight technology marketplace.

The CTO as Change Agent

Internal IT organizations ultimately have to be better vendors than the external vendors who can replace them. This means providing a higher level of targeted service with a well-defined set of core competencies at the best cost. The key to this process is hiring good employees and then asking hard questions. There is no substitute, especially in this economic climate, for hiring fewer, better skilled staff and giving them greater responsibility.

But skills are not the only requirement. An openness to change and a culture that emphasizes continuous improvement are critical to meeting the goal of an organization that is always moving forward. The key role for the CTO in this organization is to help be an agent of change, to get the best people in the right positions and to build a culture of open accountability, where there are no givens and everyone is free to question the status quo. Trust and true delegation of authority are critical to the success of this type of open organization.

How does a chief technology officer gain the knowledge to provide leadership and strategic thinking and add value to the business? There is no substitute for experience. A technical background is a must, but perhaps more important is a business or marketing background. The true test of any business initiative is how well it adds to the company's bottom line, rather than being an "interesting technology."

Many CTOs today pursue technological solutions, either blind to or unwilling to see their implications for the business. Numerous examples exist of companies that are over-provisioned, over-staffed, and building IT systems to solve non-existent business problems. Keeping abreast of technological change boils down to a few good habits:

Keep an open door.

The first and most important habit is the willingness to be open to new ideas. Every CTO needs to devote time and energy to talking with potential new vendors or partners to understand the next generation of technological or service innovations. This also extends to actively and aggressively seeking out your peers to understand how they are applying technology to their business and the value it brings.

Keep an open book.

As part of this background, it takes a lot of reading to understand the business and technical landscape. Keeping open to new ideas is a must for success. A healthy skepticism and a focus on fewer but deeper partnerships also help to shape where time is spent and resources allocated.

Keep an open mind.

Staying close to your employees and partners and asking lots of questions will bring you much closer to your organization and its needs.

Keep an open dialog.

Understand and continue to engage in all aspects of the business. The CTO is one of the few executives, other than the CEO, who can bring a more global, strategic perspective to the table and therefore add value.

Critical Partnerships

The CTO is confronted with an ever-changing landscape of partners and potential partners that bring new products to the market. Into this landscape a CTO must impose some order and pick key partners that will potentially make or break his business. As I mentioned, one of the most important assets a CTO must possess is an open mind. He or she must be willing to research and meet with companies and encourage his or her staff to do the same. Of course, any company requires a level of pre-qualification, but it can't be underestimated how having a breadth of knowledge of the offerings available today can make or break a business. In this way, a potentially useful new technology can be found.

How do you decide to engage in a partnership, once you've found that potential new partner? Several variables enter into this decision. Most important are the financial, business, and technology underpinnings of your potential partner:

❏ Do they have the financial and technical wherewithal to do what you expect?

❏ Can they be a reliable partner that is willing to open its business processes to you (since you will be very engaged in whatever they deliver to you)?

❏ Are their service agreements sound and enforceable?

❏ Do they have sound security practices and audits in place?

❏ How scalable is their service?

❏ What internal systems do they have to do billing, CRM, provisioning, monitoring, and problem tracking or resolution?

❏ What are their response time guarantees from the Helpdesk, and how is it staffed?

Perhaps most important to evaluating a vendor or partner is speaking with customers who can provide references. You must be able to contact some current customers and gauge their satisfaction with the vendor and their ability to deliver. Vitally important are the existing partnerships and types of partnerships engaged by your vendor. If it is dependent on a third party that does not meet your standards, this can lead to unexpected consequences.

Be open to looking at technologies that are outside the norm, but remember all the hard questions above. There can be a significant competitive advantage for a company that adopts a new technology or service before their competition can engage.

Challenge Your Vendors

The risk that every company runs in an outsourced relationship is to not pay attention to that relationship. Every partner has to represent a significant investment of time and understanding to ensure that your needs and agreements are being met. That's why the concept of fewer strategic partners is so critical. Outsourcing across numerous vendors, all performing similar activities, only leads to duplicated effort, loss of focus, and ultimately failures caused by lack of coordination and communication. I cannot emphasize enough the concept of picking a few strategic vendors and being heavily involved in their business at all levels to enhance your own business.

Another critical aspect of a vendor relationship is to ask the hard questions, some of which I've mentioned. But every partnership involves continuously exploring vendor performance, evaluating agreements, reviewing both operational and financial metrics, and most importantly, exploring new or expanded product development efforts.

Customers are your best method for understanding where vendors need to innovate. Invite your partners in to understand your needs and business better, and then work with them in improving or creating services that expand the relationship. This will give you even greater leverage in the relationship, along with meeting your needs even more closely.

We now live in a very interconnected, partner-driven world. No single company, no matter its resources, can provide all the services required to operate its business. Each company must decide its core value proposition and discover the major inflection points for its customers. Companies can then proceed to build those key partnerships with the leaders in the technologies they require, while using state-of-the-art practices to improve their own core competencies. In line with this is the possibility of large economies of scale realized by using partners that drive down your staffing and infrastructure costs.

Doug Cavit has served as chief information officer for McAfee.com since July 1999. Since that time, he has led McAfee.com's IT and Web strategy, developing the site into one of the world's 50 most-visited Web destinations.

From 1995 to 1999, Mr. Cavit served as director of information technology for Network Associates, Inc. Before that, Mr. Cavit held posts as director of IT for Trinzic Corporation and director of technical services for Halliburton. Mr. Cavit received his B.S. degree in geophysics and his master's degree in geology from the University of California at Riverside.

THE CLASS STRUGGLE AND THE CTO

DAN WOODS

Capital Thinking

Chief Technology Officer

The Role of the CTO

A CTO is there to guarantee that the business value results from the investment in technology. The idea is that if you are in the CTO role, your job is not just to develop technology, but also to ask why you are developing that technology and why it fits into the business. You have to do the best job you can of making sure the technology development meets the business end. I would distinguish a CTO from a CIO in the following ways. I think CIOs are primarily oriented toward operations, toward running and integrating existing solutions to serve the needs of the business. A CTO's job is generally to develop some new technology either as a product or as a proprietary advantage for the company.

A myriad of obstacles stand in the way of success for a CTO. The first problem is that we love engineering and technology so much that we forget why we are being paid. We are not being paid to build cool stuff. We are paid, rather, to build systems that will help our customers or make our companies run better. A programmer grows up and becomes a CTO when he or she starts thinking more about the business than the technology.

The second obstacle is the marginalization of technology work. In some senses, technology is similar to the arts of knitting, crocheting, and lace-making. It is interesting, valuable, and fiendishly complex – in short, a Byzantine world unto itself. It is valued by the world but is not central to success. Many CTOs will hate the idea that technology is not central, but it isn't. We all know companies with horrible technology that have great businesses. Anyone who has worked hands-on with AOL's Rainmaker page-building system can testify to that, but AOL bought Time Warner, despite Rainmaker's shortcomings. On the other hand, many companies with brilliant technology have utterly failed. The marginalization of the details of technology is an obstacle to success because it frequently means that a CTO doesn't have a seat at the table when core business strategy is being discussed. Technology makes a difference when it is married with a vision for how it can create value for a business. A CTO understands a business when he or she can put to work those knitters and lace-makers whom nobody understands to make something that, combined with the right organization and management, will make customers happy and crush the competition. Does anybody want to know about the details, even then? No, that's why it's an art. What people care about is how good the company looks in its new clothes.

The third obstacle to success as a CTO is that once we get a seat at the table, we are unprepared for battle. Other executives don't want to talk to us because we frequently answer questions by descending into what we know – technology – instead of speaking in terms that others can understand. If we can talk, then we frequently don't spend the time learning the basics of finance, accounting, sales, and marketing, so we can participate in the discussion. Finally, as a class, we are politically inept. We generally disdain "politics" as if it can be ignored. It can't. Politics is simply putting the best face on your argument, getting your story out to convince others of your views, and making things happen in an organization. A CTO prepared for battle can be a powerful force to help a company succeed.

Measuring Success as a CTO

The measures of success must be stated in terms of the business value being created by the investment in technology. You can measure this much the same way you measure the performance of any division. Are they performing their duties on time, on budget, without disruption to the rest of the organization? Have processes improved after the deployment of a system? Are we making more money? You can apply a variety of other metrics, such as uptime, speed of page delivery, and adherence to service level agreements. Good organizations provide a lot of metrics on software development process – for example, bugs found, bugs fixed, number of changes processed through a change control process, and number of lines of code written in a certain week. None of those metrics is sufficient to tell a very comprehensive story, but together, they can be used to run the business more effectively.

There is a more intangible measure of success for a CTO. Do other executives want to ask him or her questions? Are they smarter about what technology can and cannot do and how much it costs to do certain things because of his involvement? Does the CTO participate in sales and investment presentations? In short, is he an important player in the organization? The more so, the better.

There are many different ways to be successful as a CTO. Anybody's management style is really a reflection of his or her personality. Common characteristics of CTOs who will build creative teams are people who hire well, who delegate, who create a sense of ownership in the team they are leading for the work they are doing, and who have the ability to encourage a culture of cooperation, as opposed to a culture of fear. Another quality I would point to is the ability to be a strong advocate and salesman, to communicate what the department will deliver to the rest of the company, and to justify the resources that are needed to perform that function. Also, a vital factor is the ability to excel at tasks that are natural weaknesses for engineers, such as estimating time and cost. Engineers tend to be optimistic people who are rewarded for saying, "Yes, I can do that." Underestimation is the most frequent mistake in software development.

CTOs have the best chance to succeed as a force in a company when they see themselves as people who are in the business of making technology work to meet the goals of the company, not in the technology business for its own sake. The more everybody in the technology organization thinks about the basic structure of the business, the better synchronized the technology department will be. One of the mistakes engineers frequently make is fascination with technology for its own sake. The CTO has to protect the company from this habit. The world is littered with brilliant technology that did not ensure the success of businesses, and very good businesses run on weak technology. Technology is not sufficient to ensure the success of a business, and sometimes it's not necessary.

The key leadership skill is the ability to understand the needs of those who are not technologists, to cross the barriers and navigate the bridges between engineering and business. CTOs can travel in both worlds; they can have both a business discussion and an engineering discussion. CTOs have communications skills and are able to understand how to communicate with people who are not technical. One of the biggest skills is being able to select and build teams that are empowered to do creative work. Leadership in technology is a matter of setting forth healthy principles that will encourage the success of everyone in the organization, as well as the organization as a whole, and behaving consistently with respect to those principles. You want to appeal to principles, not authority.

94

The ability to hire people who are emotionally secure and humble about technology's role in a company is critical. Then you must listen to them and empower them. The result will be a fabulous team who will work hard and improve each other's skills for the thrill of it. This will lead to an environment of trust, where people will listen to each other, because they're not looking to constantly dominate or make up for their own insecurities. That's the key to team building – hiring people who are comfortable with themselves and who understand the goal of technology.

Determining the Best Technologies to Use

Knowing how the technology is going to fit in as part of a comprehensive solution and knowing what kinds of problems you will encounter in the implementation and how you will address them are the keys to selecting technology. No technology ever solves all problems comprehensively. The best thing to do is evaluate a technology with respect to its weaknesses. The goal should be to bring to the surface the ugly truth about what life will be like using that technology. If your organization is highly able to handle the problems inherent in the technology you choose, you've probably made a good fit. If you've chosen a technology, and you don't know what kind of problems to expect with it, then you've probably made a mistake.

With respect to choosing between building, buying, and open source, I don't think there are really any rules, because the business situations vary so much. Sometimes it makes sense to buy the top of the line; sometimes it makes sense to buy what is just good enough. Sometimes development is the right choice, although I recommend a high hurdle for internally developing a solution. You should do so only if the benefits will be huge and when you have the ability to make a sustained investment in a team for development and support.

The Technologically Nimble Company

In a properly managed company there is room to think, what author and management guru Tom DeMarco calls "slack." People have time to experiment and keep up with technology. In the dot-com craze, too many organizations were run at full tilt all the time, and in those cases, nobody could keep up because they were just barely able to do what they were supposed to be doing. You also want to make training and personal skill development valued by the company. Finally, I think there should be proof-of-concept projects that allow people to take short breaks from their activities to create small prototypes that allow new technology to be understood.

In terms of specific technologies, I think functional languages like Lisp have proven themselves highly productive and valuable in a variety of business situations. The Yahoo Stores are based on Lisp. It's a little known fact, but when MS Windows starts up, a Prolog interpreter is involved. One study comparing Lisp, Java, and C++ showed that Lisp is one of the most productive ways to write software. Although it's not a technology, specifically, the ASP trend, the economics of hosted applications enabled by some of the Web services, will be an unstoppable force in the marketplace. Managed services, the ability to outsource a complex technical function, such as firewall management, will be an important thing. I don't think anyone has it exactly right at the moment, but as time goes on, it will be a tremendous cost advantage to the people who are intelligent about providing and using such services.

We're now in a period of digestion, as opposed to a period of innovation. People will find many ways to use existing technology more effectively, even simple things like e-mail and file-sharing across the Web. All of these things will now be merged with organizational processes. The rapid innovation in technology will finally be caught up with by the ability of companies to change the way they do business to create the efficiency that was always the goal.

When there is constantly a gap between what a vendor says they will deliver and what they actually do, it's a big warning sign. All the traditional signals are important, such as happy customers, which are a tremendous endorsement. It is also important to make sure the vendor's management is stable and that they have some proven expertise in the area in which they are claiming to solve problems. They should have experience; the answer to every question shouldn't be "yes"; and they should be more than willing to talk about the weaknesses of their software. If I could evaluate a company on only one question, it would be "What is your core competency?" If you ask that over and over again to everyone in a company and get the same answer, that's probably a pretty good company.

Specifically, I'm really persuaded that the rapid development cycle methodologies, such as eXtreme Programming and Scrum and a variety of other techniques, have it right in that they recognize that it is impossible to predict and design in the abstract a system that will be successful. A better plan is to build a system, place it in the hands of users, and then listen to what they say. That is one of the most important lessons of the last five years of Internet development. Launch 75 percent of what you think the customer needs, and then pay attention and rev the product very rapidly based on user input. This development methodology is enabled by the network, because you can't do that if you have to have people installing new software all the time, but you can do it if the software is served from a central location.

Evaluating Risk

The risks you take as a CTO should match your personal investment portfolio. The bulk of your time should be invested in low-risk projects that meet the core needs of the business. Maybe 5 percent of your portfolio should be in speculative projects that could be worth either nothing or a huge amount in five years. This means that it is appropriate to bet on an unproven technology or method when there is essentially a low impact and a high payoff. You don't want to take a risk of having your core infrastructure fall apart, but if you never experiment, you probably aren't learning fast enough.

One of the weaknesses of technologists is that they get fascinated with cool technology, and you really have to ask yourself if they're taking a risk for fun or because the business payoff is good. If you find yourself fascinated and obsessed with the possibilities of a technology, post a note on your bulletin board reminding yourself to constantly check that the business value is always there.

We have a CTO Club in New York City that has saved the membership millions of dollars' worth of mistakes. The best way to keep your edge is to regularly talk to your peers about what problems they are worried about and what they are doing to solve them. Reading about new

97

technologies helps, but you also have to play around and make sure you still have a hands-on feel about how long it takes to do things. I encourage people to play around with new technologies.

Best Advice

The best advice I've received is to ask what the business justification is for the technology you're being asked to build or support. People who are engineers are rewarded most of their careers for saying, "Yes, I can do that." They're not encouraged to ask why they're doing what they're asked to do. As an engineer, the more you ask why, in business terms, you're being asked to do a certain technology project, and the more you're part of that discussion, the better it is for you, and the better it is for the business.

Most of the problems that exhibit themselves in technology development occur because of poor estimating skills on everybody's part, from the management to the programmers and on down. The advice I give is to recognize that there's a difference between thinking something through and actually doing it. If I gave you a pad of paper filled with numbers on every page and asked you to add all those numbers and get the answer, you could think through it in a minute, but actually adding them all up would take you a week. That's the biggest systemic problem with technology development. People confuse the time it takes to think things through with the time it takes to do things properly.

Future Considerations

Technology will be much more focused on providing complete solutions to business problems and much less focused on tools that are generally applied.

To sell a solution for technology in the future, you will need three things. One is a vertical knowledge of a certain business problem. Another is software you've written to enable you to solve the things you need solved to make a difference for that vertical solution. Finally, you'll have to have a hosted delivery mechanism as an option.

In another area of concern for the future, I think privacy is primarily going to be legislated from Washington, and people will react to that. People have shown little concern about privacy in the way they behave. They say they're concerned about privacy, but they don't spend the time to ensure that privacy. We don't live in a very paranoid culture. We live in a culture that is open to exchanging information. I think it's more likely that Washington will legislate privacy than people will actually demand it.

A CTO's Golden Rules

Keep your eye on the business value. The CTO's fundamental role is reducing the risk and ensuring that the investment in technology produces the appropriate business benefits. You must know why you're building what you're building. Try to make sure the business relationships you have are mutually beneficial, so that over a long period they will be supported and sustained, rather than forgotten about.

Trust is very efficient. Building trust in your employee relationships, your relationships with other parts of the company, and your relationships with your vendors will result in tremendous efficiencies. It's not easy to do, and it's sometimes made impossible by business conditions, but if you can do it, you will reap great benefits.

Dan Woods' unique combination of experience in software development, management, and journalism, focused on creating products for the Internet, has made him an essential contributor to the creation of CapitalThinking.com. Having led development and deployment for three seminal Internet sites, TheStreet.com, Pathfinder, and NandO.net, Mr. Woods has developed a dynamic, secure commercial mortgage banking Web site to support the operations of the company.

Formerly vice president and chief technology officer of TheStreet.com, Mr. Woods is widely known among Internet cognoscenti as a pioneer in Web technology. Managing the application development of Pathfinder for Time Inc., he was responsible for launching Time Inc.'s online magazines. An award winning reporter specializing in the banking industry, he was in the vanguard of bringing the newspaper industry into the computer age.

While studying for a master's degree in journalism at Columbia, he developed, in partnership with Pulitzer Prize-winning investigative reporter Elliot Jaspin, a PC-based nine-track tape analysis software that allows reporters to gain access to government data stored on mainframe computers. Immediately after completing his bachelor's degree in computer science at the University of Michigan, Mr. Woods worked as a consultant for companies like Citibank, JP Morgan, and Hewitt Associates, developing financial analysis systems, fourth-generation language interpreters, and benefit management systems. Mr. Woods is the author, with Tom Snee and Larne Pekowsky, of A Developer's Guide to the Java Web Server.

INSIDE THE JOB: A CTO'S PERSPECTIVE ON THE ROLE OF A CTO

MIKE TOMA

eLabor

Chief Technology Officer

The Role of the CTO

Ask a group of CTOs what their role is in their respective organizations, and the answers will be as varied as each of the companies. This is one of the biggest industry debates since the title was established in the early 1990s. The reality is that the role will vary across companies and industries, depending on its focus and the corporate maturity level. Generally, the CTO responsibilities and tasks will span the levels from strategic to tactical and operational within an organization. Today, most CTOs will handle some combination of these responsibilities for their organizations. Another way to look at it is that CTOs may have bottom- or top-line responsibility, or both, in addition to the technology vision for the company.

From my perspective the CTO, as the title implies, should be an officer in the company with strategic and operational responsibilities in addition to setting technology vision. The technology vision in the company has to be tied directly into other corporate strategies, so the CTO can be more effective in his role. This is most common in small- to medium-sized organizations.

My role as CTO at eLabor is to run the technical operations of the business. As part of the executive management team, I ensure that both the operations of my divisions and the technology vision are in alignment with the business strategies of the company. I'm involved with Sales & Marketing, Business Development, and Professional Services to bridge the gap between the technology and other business-oriented groups in the company.

Technical companies need to focus on using technology as a tool to leverage business strategies, rather than focusing on the technology strategy as the business. This is the key role for the CTO – to be strategic rather than tactical. Without this, the CTO becomes just a technologist, deciding on one technology over another, which is more in line with the traditional CIO model.

Judging Success

Success or failure of a CTO is usually pretty obvious. Each of us looks to the obvious indicators of success such as the success of the business. Is the data center operating at 100 percent availability or meeting its service level agreements? Do we have happy and satisfied customers? Are products being delivered on time? Is product quality high? Are we meeting the expectations of the customers?

These types of indicators are all standard fare for the tactical operations of the business. From a senior manager or strategic perspective, certainly feedback from the CEO is important, but I think what's more important is whether the CTO is determining strategies or are the strategies being determined for him. The CTO should be actively involved in creating strategies, not just being there to execute on them. To me this is the one indicator of whether the CTO is capable of fulfilling a strategic role in the organization. Putting all these things together helps me gauge how I am doing as a CTO.

Additionally, for CTOs to be successful, they must be able to communicate at all levels in the organization. They must be able to talk at different levels, whether they are in front of engineers or in the boardroom. A CTO's knowledge and expertise needs to cover the same cross section. CTOs must be good managers and technologists, but it is critical that they understand the business model. This is the most important skill to be able to bridge the gap between business and technology.

Generally, the normal operational situations, such as keeping the data center running, getting the phone call that something crashed and is down, being able to produce and deliver product on demand with a minimum of resources, and trying to balance quality and speed, are all things that worry CTOs.

However, the biggest worries are usually in areas such as balancing your time between strategic and operational priorities and setting proper expectations.

Technology Selection and Execution

My strategy for technology advancement is to map out a broad technology strategy that is high-level and directional in nature. Within this roadmap, I tend to rely on my key technologists in different areas and use them to experiment and prototype different things. Specific direction and decisions come out of meetings the team has to review the benefits of a particular technology or direction. This group isn't a formal committee, but an assembly of key personnel, whose decisions are based on consensus. Everyone must express an opinion and either agree based on their views or go along with the majority after discussing their opposing views. As CTO, I make the final decisions and mediate disagreements.

Our strategy for weeding out cool versus useful technologies is very simple. Our process and culture enable creativity and experimentation. People don't have a lot of time because of deadlines and workloads, so we quickly go through and either prototype or play with a new technology. If it doesn't seem to have a quick enough ROI, or barriers to entry are too high, then we typically drop it. I encourage my key individuals to try things on the side and see whether they are useful. Cool technologies usually fall out because there is just not enough time.

Execution strategies of these new technologies are a tricky business. My preference is to support more of an evolutionary execution model than a revolutionary one. I believe incremental growth and adoption is a better business strategy and therefore better for the business. A perfect illustration to support this was the success and failures of our execution strategy of new technologies in 1996 and 1999.

In 1996, we jumped into the JAVA wave and threw caution to the wind. We had many struggles and problems with it because it was a new technology. Generally, it cost us a lot of resources and 18 months to completely reengineer one of our product lines. We encountered a large number of problems, but basically we tied up the resources and lost the use of the new product until it was launched almost two years later.

In 1999, our business strategy changed to an ASP model. At that time, we had to decide to take basically a first-generation product over to

JAVA IIEE and JAVA beans or completely switch gears again, based on the right technology for the strategic direction of our business. In the end, for many reasons including the technology, we chose to move to the Microsoft Tools platform. This time we also decided to change our execution strategy because of the problems encountered in the switch to Java. We didn't put a lot of money in it and completely rewrite everything; we decided to take an evolutionary approach instead. We would take one component, design it, prototype it, develop it, and release it as a mixed or combined technology. That worked very well for us. We essentially had 60- to 90-day release cycles that allowed us to produce higher quality product, as well as shift directions based on technological hurdles and customer feedback. It still took us 18 months to get through everything, but we had a better quality product, and we were able to use the product in the market the whole time.

We have latched onto this success and will continue down this path because it enables us to conduct business and at the same time introduce new technology easily with minimum risk. Now moving to the next-generation .NET strategy, we will follow the same process – incrementally replacing components or modules with the .NET infrastructure one at a time. This will enable us to learn the new technology and reduce the risk to the business.

Technology as a Strategic Advantage

Being technologically nimble is a mindset. It must be part of the culture. We have defined ourselves as leading-edge. We aren't necessarily bleeding edge – we used to be, but we have backed off from that quite a bit. Our current culture is that we accept new technologies and intend to focus on them fairly early in their life cycle. This culture helps motivate people to continue reading about new technologies and encourages them to learn, try new things, and discuss them among the teams. While we may not necessarily adopt the new technologies right away, people are exposed to them and learn to understand the business metrics driving such decisions.

This culture is important in retaining the best technologists. If your culture keeps people from wanting training or learning new technologies, you will have mediocre people and be way behind the curve. I believe it's best to encourage learning behavior and adopt new technologies when they fit the business strategy or, at worst, don't detract from or risk it.

The overall business strategy for technology is to either be more competitive or to reduce costs. By reducing costs, we end up being quicker to market and ultimately become more competitive, as well. These are the kinds of things we focus on and evaluate to leverage technology decisions to be more competitive. As a technology leader in the organization, the CTO must exercise control over the areas that can have an impact. Making decisions on which technology should be used to get a product out to market more quickly and which technologies have lower overhead costs and shorter development cycles, etc., will all have an impact on our being more competitive in the market. Technologies, processes, architectures, and many other areas also need to be considered for getting to market more quickly and getting the features faster. These are things we focus on in making decisions across the board, particularly in technology.

Future Tech, Fantasy Tech

I think the degree of technology innovation is directly related to the economy and the flow of investment money. As an impact from the current economic slowdown, I think technological innovation over the next two to three years will be at the lowest levels we've seen in some time. There will always be some level of innovation, but articles in trade publications give you a sense for how much of it is out there. These magazines have not been reporting on too many new technologies lately.

I am fairly optimistic, but in looking at technology and the industry in the current climate, I tend to favor a more pessimistic outlook over the next three to five years. I believe there will not be much revolutionary change in the short term. I think the makeup of markets will shift as they always do. Revenue and growth pressures will cause consolidations and changes in the market to satisfy these needs. There will be some new players in various industries that are born but, by and large, the industry will generate the same solutions. I don't believe there will be many revolutionary changes; I think we generally will see the normal market cycling.

The Internet wave has died down after the big bang of the dot-com era. I believe there are a few areas that right now have potential for standing out over the next few years. Web services have the potential for a lot of play in the industry. Backed by some major players such as Microsoft, IBM, Sun, HP, and others, the Web services concept based on an XML and SOAP standard has the ability to get mind share in the next few years. It should succeed because ubiquitous integration is one of the biggest headaches of everyone in the industry. It provides a promise of being something the industry can get behind with a lot of momentum, which will cause more companies to jump on the bandwagon and support it. This is important because normal business cycles around new technology are to wait through the big bang press and initial momentum to see if it lasts before there is widespread adoption. If there is a big enough push for Web services, then people will get behind it and use XML and SOAP protocols that are being pushed to standard.

Wireless is another area that still has a lot of upside potential. We are basically still in the infancy stage of the market, and as communication levels improve, this will become one of the more important technologies in the industry. I think we'll see evolution in the wireless device markets, but once technology and communications improve, there will be an explosion in the phone devices. The key to this is that there are millions of educated users of phone devices, versus quite a few people needing to learn how to use a PDA. We'll see much more application and services around voice or touch recognition on phone devices.

Generally, I see the standard evolution in wireless networking, but no great leaps within this area. We'll also see more technologies to help aggregate data to different devices and media. In the long term, one of the hottest areas will be the use of nano technology.

If I could create any new technology for our future, I would pick a technology that automatically developed technology. I don't want to get rid of the software engineers and designers, but it would be nice to be able to manufacture a technology "black box" that automatically manufactures technology based on some specifications without bugs or problems. Some of the biggest problems we deal with day in and day out are in the design, development, and testing process of producing products.

Online Privacy and Security

To me, privacy and security are two different things. Privacy is the protection from disclosure of information; whereas, security is securing of systems and data. I tend to look at privacy in terms of people using the Internet to do e-commerce types of activities. Capturing and protecting information are the underpinnings of privacy issues and are the focus of many in the industry. I don't have a lot of involvement in this area, other than to have an opinion as a consumer. I believe my information and online habits should be protected from general distribution.

Security is the focus of securing corporate or customer data. Security is a critical element of our business because we sell and host mission-critical applications for our customers. We have adopted a very strict policy, and we try to take it to the extreme to protect the data and systems. We lock down everything first and open areas only if there is an urgent need. This is the key to our policy, but we do all the other standard techniques for things such as virus scanning to denial of service detection.

A good security policy requires you to intimately know the underlying technology. E-mail is an example of an area that tends to have numerous security vulnerabilities. Our policy is that we don't allow inbound e-mail traffic into our data center. This approach eliminates the risk, rather than minimizing it. We will shut down every hole in the firewall except HTTP traffic. We take a much stricter control over what we do with our systems. We can do this because we have the ability to focus our product development efforts on solutions that don't use these areas of vulnerability. We have the flexibility and control to make those decisions and then do something about it.

Due Diligence on Acquisitions

We've made six or seven acquisitions in the past three years, so I have a lot of experience in due diligence. Due diligence strategies vary, depending on the length of time available to perform them. There are four fundamental strategies, however, that should be followed, regardless of the cycle time of the process. Your assessment of an acquisition target should focus on the business strategy, product strategy, technology/ architecture strategy, and organizational/people strategy.

The first step is understanding the business strategy behind the acquisition. What is the target of the combined entity? What are the limitations or influences, such as cost, timing, and resources to achieve the target strategy? A CTO must understand these fundamental expectations and constraints to properly assess whether the acquisition can meet those business objectives.

Assessing the product strategy helps you understand where a product fits in the market and where the company intended to take it. Questions to dive into include: What are the features of the product? Who are the users? What is the competitive analysis of the product? How is it sold? Who are the buyers? Who are the users? What's their understanding of the market? Making sure that the product strategy fits or is close enough for adaptation to the overall direction is critical.

The technology and architecture assessment is focused on understanding what technologies are used to create the product and how its architecture fits in relation to your own products. It's important to gauge the level of sophistication of the product to determine the stability, reusability, and maintenance of the source. Information gathered in these assessments will be used to determine how good a fit the product has in relation to your products and, to some extent, the scope of the effort to close the gap between technologies and architectures.

The final analysis is of the people and organizational structure of the company. You need to assess how the company is operating. How have they organized their business? How are they producing products? What's their culture? During this phase I am usually trying to assess the risk for the underlying foundation of the product and the scope for the new combined entity to be able to accomplish the new business objectives. Much of this information will be used to shape the post-acquisition strategy and plan.

After taking all of the evaluations into consideration, there has to be better than an 80 percent fit to continue moving forward.

Best Business Advice

The one piece of advice I've received that really stands out is, "Business is not about the best technology or product. It is about the fundamentals of business and making money." As technologists, we tend to want to do things the best way, do things properly, and create the best product. I was given this advice early in my career, but it is something you really have to learn, as a technologist, through experience. Technology and product are important in themselves, but it is more important to have sound business principles in the other business organizations to support the business. This is hard for technologists and product people to swallow because they feel what they do is the most important. And it probably sounds funny coming from a CTO.

What I have found is that you don't need the best product or features to have a good business strategy. There are many examples in the industry of companies that have good business models without the best product. Conversely, there are many examples of failed businesses that had the best technologies or products but lacked many business fundamentals. I have come to embrace this concept as a CTO because I am responsible for balancing business and technology strategies and not allowing developers and technologists to always create the ultimate solution – it just needs to be good enough.

Golden Rules for the CTO

One of the golden rules for being a CTO is to be honest on all fronts. You have to be the reality person in the organization. There are many times when you are out there, pushing and pitching with the rest of them, but when it comes down to it, you still need to be the reality check for what the company can or can't do at all levels.

In addition to being realistic and honest, a CTO must be a good leader. You need to set the example. Being a good leader means you need to be at all levels, dealing with technology, people, and business strategies. You need to avail yourself to all parts of the organization, so you get that buy in.

Named CTO of eLabor in 1997, Mike Toma oversees strategic planning for software development, corporate information technology, and data center operations. As a corporate officer, he is responsible for influencing the company's strategic direction and aligning technology with the company's vision, goals, and objectives. This includes leveraging technology to create new and enhanced revenue opportunities, as well as creating a competitive advantage to deliver products and services.

In May 2001, Mr. Toma was appointed to the CTO Advisory Council for InfoWorld magazine, in which he participates in editorial projects. Mr. Toma is also the founder of the Los Angeles CTO Forum, a peer group organization dedicated to providing CTOs with a forum to interact and discuss business and technology interests.

With a career spanning 14 years in the software industry, Mr. Toma has held various positions in the industry as a consultant, software engineer, business analyst, software development manager, product manager, and VP of operations.

Mr. Toma performed his undergraduate work in computer science at California State University, Northridge.

POSITIONING TECHNOLOGY SOLUTIONS TO ADDRESS BUSINESS NEEDS

MICHAEL S. DUNN

Encoda Systems

Chief Technology Officer, Executive Vice President

The Role of the CTO

For most of the last ten years, I've been acting in the role of a CTO, even before the title was en vogue. I have a background as a developer and have been interested in computers since I was a teenager, even before the dawn of PCs. I was lucky enough to be able to participate in some of what was going on in universities at the time, primarily because my father was teaching at a university. I was able to work with the computer department at the university where he was teaching, which gave me some exposure to computers at a much younger age than my peers. After that early exposure, I knew where I wanted to go with my career. I saw computer technology as a way to leverage my interest in both creative and analytical ventures – or put simply, to use both sides of my brain. I worked on developing a computer engineering focus and tended to be drawn to both the hardware and the software aspects of technology. I started my paid experience doing what used to be called programming, but which is now commonly called being a developer. I was a part of a wide variety of application development efforts, from traditional mainframe and midrange structured coding, to real-time processing and was especially interested in AI during its heyday earlier in my career. I became exposed and interested in the many diverse ways to do development, rather than just focusing on the top down structure mainframe-based development most programmers were focusing on. I also liked learning about the whole system instead of just having one specific area of focus. That diverse knowledge also opened up to me a few unique job opportunities working closely with business leaders while I was fairly early in my career. As such, I had to learn a lot about the businesses in order to implement the proper technologies, either as a team or as a leader. I was thrown willingly into management at a very young age and very early into my career. I especially liked learning about the business drivers to success, and then positioning the technology solutions to address those needs. I liked building technology solutions, but I also liked building the teams that supported them. That diverse background, in both business and technology leadership roles, rounded out my early career and set the direction towards what ultimately became a CTO role as we know it today.

From my perspective, CTOs are technology leaders who are tasked with guiding a company's effort to meet business objectives via technology initiatives. So even though it has technology within the title, and you're driving technology projects and leading technology teams, you're building solutions that meet business objectives first and foremost. You have to be very in tune with the direction of your company, so that you can proactively provide technology that supports and extends your business initiatives. If you don't have this focus, you're likely to do technology projects simply for technology's sake, and that's a disastrous and wasteful thing to do in business. It's neither productive nor cost-effective.

Again, the job of a CTO is to meet business objectives via technology. It is commonly the role of the most senior technology leader in the company. The CTO is almost always the lead technologist for the company, depending on what your company does. Sometimes they are a peer to the CIO, and the CIO might do more backend or operational tasks, while the CTO might do more front-end, customer focused tasks. The CTO also touches the product, touches the consumer, and touches the business partner. It is a strategic role. Sometimes the CTO will work for the CIO, but it usually works best the other way around, with the CIO internally focused and the CTO focusing on the external.

The CTO is the leader of a technology group or unit, and one aspect of that role is internal information technology, commonly lead by a CIO. The technology leader should manage that role as well. The CTO has to be a strong leader, almost evangelical, and have very good collaborative and communicative skills. One of the more difficult tasks is translating complex technologies into concepts and ideas that business leaders will understand, even if they aren't technically savvy beyond the management of their laptops. They have to be able to understand and apply these ideas to what they do for a living, whether they head marketing, sales, or finance units. There is a translation side to these management-level discussions.

In some regards, CTOs act as guides, both internally and externally. They are almost always the external voice for the company around technology direction or partnerships. Often the CTO owns the technical due diligence side of merger and acquisition activities or investments. In this regard, they help shape the organic growth and strategic direction of the company.

Success as a CTO

I classify CTOs into two groups: "I" CTOs and "we" CTOs. This is analogous to the way they speak. I, for example, consider myself a "we" CTO. "We" CTOs tend to build teams, and in their conversations, though they'll use the word "I" when they're really acknowledging that something occurred or they led something, it's always "we" with regard to the actual entity responsible for some activity.

"I" CTOs tend to be founding CTOs of a company or its chief scientists, and they are constantly speaking in terms of "I think we should do this" or "I think we should do that." They are close to what I would call futurists, in that they are almost always thinking in terms of pure strategy.

"We" CTOs tend to build things and own both technical and strategic responsibilities. They understand that to build something and move it forward takes groups of people. Their job is to build teams to mentor, teach, and guide. At the same time, they have to be very good listeners, because they aren't just gaining insight into direction through their own thoughts and research, but rather by gathering numerous inputs and coming to a collective conclusion. It is through the aggregate thoughts and ideas of the teams they lead and those they peer or partner with that they gain insight. Listening skills are incredibly important in how I view the CTO role. The "I" CTO roles are not uninteresting, but I am personally, consciously drawn toward "we" types of CTO roles.

As a CTO, you need to create an environment that allows you to track metrics around everything you do. The most important metric for a CTO is an understanding of how to gauge a project's return on investment. A CTO constantly recommends to the company the investment side, and it has to go toward supporting a revenue stream, which is the return side. You cannot get there through a subjective view of doing a project simply because it's cool or because everyone else is doing it. Justification has to be objective: Making a certain level of investment and using this type of technology will give us this revenue stream or this efficiency that we are looking for. The return does not have to be purely financial; it can be a cost savings or efficiency in the way you're doing business. Having a good handle on the metrics that drive your business will help you efficiently create a functional ROI model for your technology unit.

Change is constant in technology. It is important to understand your framework for technology – the architectures you have chosen as your standards, the supporting processes, and the teams that leverage them. A known framework gives you the ability to quickly gauge whether a new edition that is offered from the technology industry is valid, such as a new tool or a new process or a new application. Each might be able to fill a gap in your framework for you, but if it's wrong, it might distract you.

This constant assessment of new offerings against a framework is probably the only way you won't be frenetically changing what you are doing and can maintain some sense of sanity. You have to be able to tie offerings together and quickly ascertain whether what has just come out is applicable or not. This discipline is important not only for you, but also for your team; otherwise, your team will constantly want to do the latest and greatest just because it is. Unless you're on the bleeding edge of the industry, this is probably something you should stay away from.

You look toward the basics in every technology you analyze: stability, scalability, and feature functionality. If you don't have a good sense of where you are today and what you need to progress, you won't be able to accurately gauge whether what just became available is applicable or not. If you're doing technology for technology's sake, you'll want to be up with the latest trend, but you'll end up being very reactive. You want to be proactive. You want to be in a position where you're not surprised by new technology because you're so in tune with what the industry is doing. You can take note of what is new and then move forward.

Keeping Technologically Nimble

One of the biggest challenges for any CTO is staying technologically nimble. Creating a nimble organization starts with your structure, management bench strength, raw technological manpower, and efficient developmental and operational methodologies, which are all pulled together via a commonly understood framework. The entire organization needs to be aware of and part of touch points, the technology unit's overall methodology. This requires constant communication and statements of a direction regarding the efforts your technology unit is undertaking to meet the business objectives.

Business, in general, is filled day-to-day with ambiguity. On the technology front, ambiguity has been the norm for quite a while. Systems have been getting more robust, more modular, and more componentized. While this creates extreme efficiencies, with it comes complexity, such as with very dynamic environments created by component-based development. If you are tied to a known framework, and you've set that vision toward your tools and your methodologies, and your metrics allow you to track your scope and progress, then you'll have created good visibility in both your projects and your overall ability to support the needs of the business. Even though your teams are doing very complex projects, if you've created good visibility, you can be proactive in your approach. You won't have to be reactive to figure out halfway into a project that some element is failing; you can take corrective action at every potential stumbling point. If you have visibility and communication throughout your team, and if you've chosen the right framework, architectures, and tools, as well as staffed yourself with specialists who are experts in all of these areas, your team, by design, should be technologically nimble.

Of course, some projects don't naturally lend themselves to the concept of being nimble, and some conservative companies view being nimble as changing course midstream, a practice that should be avoided at all cost. Unfortunately, I think that practice fosters solutions that end up either under-delivering or missing the ultimate business objective or intended market. I personally like the idea of a team being able to deal with technological ambiguity, while not straying from the original goal of the organization.

The proper implementation of technology can create efficiencies, save costs, and contribute to revenue, while failures during the implementation phase often doom the inherent value of the overall effort, especially if the use of technology is directly related to the production of a product. In this case, producing a product by using technology is directly tied to the profitability of a company.

With respect to technology directions, I think there is huge potential in the area of Web services for the future. Web services give you the ability to outsource or garner aspects of an overall project via best-of-breed solution providers using an ASP model, which allows you to fill a certain aspect of your overall solution and gain from the ability to pick and choose what your company provides and what the Web service providers contribute. You have to take into account technological complexities to integrate all of it together, and I do believe we are in the infancy of our ability to take advantage of these services, but the concept is very exciting.

In the role of a CTO, I think it is a good idea to look at industry directions, such as Web services, and determine whether they are applicable to existing projects, giving you the ability to push your company forward through the use of new techniques and services. You might also consider whether your company should create them, especially as a way to stimulate revenue. The ability to ASP some of what is core to your company can be very interesting. Most companies need to focus on their core intellectual property, what they really should own and what produces their core revenue streams. They may want to focus their talent and expertise on that piece that is only their intellectual property, and consider an ASP or outsourcing specialist for the non-IP aspects of their solutions. Aspects that are mundane or that they might use to run their business are often considered. They can acquire these aspects directly from another company and implement them themselves, thus licensing the solution. Or they can partner with another company that can provide an aspect of the needed solution through a Web service offering.

It's critical that you, as a CTO, determine your company's core focus, and then look toward acquiring from a company the solutions needed that are not your core, or partnering with a company to find these solutions. The ability to automate aspects of business is very important, especially when you want to create efficiencies and cost savings. Many technologies that are moving forward beneficially allow you to automate certain aspects of your business. There are many standards groups looking at ways to better use an activity across diverse systems, such as XML, or more efficiently use architectures, such as tiered platforms, redundant infrastructure, and optimized transport. For example, Jxta is focused on a way to put standards around how peer-to-peer is done, and if it is successful, it will allow us to better use bandwidth and infrastructure.

Most technologies today that are considered either on the edge or approaching the edge of the technology boundary are stressing that they'll be future-aware. If you are implementing technology today that you know will be applicable in "x" amount of time, then you will not have to reinvent the wheel. You'll be using a building-block approach. A lot of component-based development for component- or module-based infrastructure deployment takes advantage of a building-block approach to a full system development. If you're constantly future-aware, you're constantly looking for technologies that extend your model, thus allowing you to extend your framework via the latest integrated technologies.

Managing Risk

As a CTO, you have to create a culture that assesses risk at the start of every project. You're constantly trying to solve a problem or produce a solution, and from both you have a certain objective that you state across the team. Your team then needs to look out across the technology landscape, see what's available toward meeting your objective, and then make your initial choices.

A team approach is always the best method of managing risk because, in my experience, many intellects and their diverse opinions are usually better than one. With an individual approach, you succeed or fail on your own merits, which, of course, some technologists like. However, when you take a team approach, you can sort out and vet the diverse opinions, and the team tends not to miss much because there's a variety of personalities and skill sets looking at the challenge and ascertaining the risk associated with it. As the CTO, you focus the team on coming to a consensus, or as much of a consensus as you can get them to; maybe you decide out of a team of ten people that eight are in agreement on an issue, and two have dissenting opinions, and that can be factored into assessing your risk. You can move forward with it from that perspective.

When you implement the plan, the most important aspect of it is a measure that constantly tracks where you actually are against that plan. You mitigate risk by tracking and paying attention to details; from there you can take corrective action as you progress along the plan. Instead of just approving and selecting a team to implement and then hoping the project will be delivered correctly at the other end, check regularly, every few weeks or once or twice a quarter, to gauge where the project is against plan and to see if it's progressing as expected.

As CTO you shouldn't have to do a lot of granular-level project management, but you do need to ensure the original expectation of the plan will be met. To succeed, a project doesn't always have to be led from the top, but it is within the team structure that you have to create methodologies that allow you to track at a granular level daily, and provide a broader oversight from time to time. This process is essential to ensure mitigation of risk.

Acting as a Leader

As a CTO, I feel you need to lead in a constructive manner. Strive to build loyalty, trust, and teamwork. The most desired traits in a CTO include the ability to listen, learn, lead, collaborate, and communicate. Those are all solid personality traits, but overall you have to have the desire to be accountable for all the technology aspects of your business. If one of your teams of developers produces something that is not successful, ultimately you failed at your job. Your job is to lead the entire effort, and you have to be willing to accept that level of responsibility. That means you're held accountable, and you take the heat if something goes south. If, however, your team produces a successful project, as the majority of the efforts should, then it's a team success. Never take sole credit for a team's success; it will destroy the credibility your have with your team.

You have to make sure that you have good partnering skills and capabilities as well. Unless your job is running a CTO organization, you're really partnering not only with whoever your customer contingency is, but with your peer business units, as well. Partnering capabilities are beneficial and necessary for a CTO.

The best CTOs I've met are those who think outside the box. Most people who get to the level of CTO have egos; it's a necessary trait. I tend to think of an ego as something for personal consumption. It's important to have a strong sense of ego for your own self-worth, but if you're laying it on too thick, and your ego is a constant presence to others around you, it's very distracting. You will not be as productive in your role as you can be. I've noticed that when people have the technical ability, intellect, and capability, they do not feel the need to be noticed constantly. What matters is what they're contributing and whether they are being good collaborators – not looking for praise. If they do something for the benefit of the company, a project, or the team, they've abandoned the issues associated with selfish intent.

Good CTOs express themselves often and aren't afraid to state an opinion, even if it's dissenting. Most situations need to have both sides raised whenever you're attempting to solve a problem. You have to be able to hear the "yes" side, but also the "no" side. Conflicting opinions can be productive when they're presented in ways that are constructive and that drive the group ultimately toward a well-rounded decision.

Earlier in my career I definitely didn't use my ego properly, and tended toward grandstanding and defensiveness. Along the way, people mentored me on the proper way to manage and to build and lead successful teams. I've had so many good mentors in my career that I've felt it's very important for me to become a mentor to those I manage, as well. It's important not only to have the ability to be taught, but also to teach. Your employees should be able to teach you and help steer you.

As my career has progressed, I have been drawn to the concept that you have to set a framework within your organization that everyone can identify with. You have to make sure they understand what is inside that framework and what is not. If they want something outside that framework, you have to create a methodology that allows new additions to the framework to be considered. You are judging whether some new piece of technology should be implemented that extends the framework. The framework doesn't have static boundaries; it's more about understanding what is in the framework and what is out of the framework – then you should assess whether to allow the new addition to change the framework. The decision needs to be very analytical.

Using the framework is actually a great way to set up a process that allows you to constantly extend your technological capabilities, and yet not break what you have already built that is successful. I have always steered my teams with this approach, and it has always been very useful to me. People understand the process: We do everything up to here; if we go beyond the framework's boundary, it's different. We're okay with being different, but let's just make sure we're not doing it for the wrong reason or breaking other areas as we go forward.

Inventing Technologies

I'm a parent, and one thing that has struck me is that the world is shrinking. It's very diverse and changing constantly right in front of my children's eyes. If I were going to develop a new piece of technology, it would actually be an extension of what we already have in Internet technologies.

My new technology would teach our children in an unbiased way about the diversity – but also the similarity – of the global community. It would educate our children to be tolerant of others, no matter what they experience in their daily environment. Children are growing up in diverse environments, and their opinions and personal direction are for the most part governed for them by their daily surroundings. Children are very impressionable. It would be a much better world if simple tolerance of others were a requirement and a given.

I don't know that there is a technology that would accomplish my goal – it's definitely a stretch – but I think it would be very worthwhile to explore. After all, technology should benefit mankind, and what a good place to start – with our children. Although there have been some negative things associated with technology from time to time, it has done a lot of positive things for the world, as well. Finding ways to positively improve our children's future should be a focus for all of us.

A CTO's Golden Rules

"Abandon religious convictions" is one of my golden rules. Often technologists get into specific technological camps and become closed-minded. They need to understand there are other viable camps out there that might be equally as good. As a CTO, you must have the ability to be agnostic about technology, because it will allow you to benefit from the entire landscape of technology, rather than just aligning yourself with one offering.

These limitations often start with an operating system or platform, such as Windows or Unix, Microsoft or Sun. They become your religious convictions, which can limit your ability to succeed. Overall, there are many diverse but great technologies available today. You have so much more freedom by being agnostic and being able to pick the best solution, no matter what the camp at any given moment. If you tie it back into a framework approach, then you aren't derailing yourself by the diversity of technology. Instead, you are logically determining and then stating that these diverse technologies contribute positively to the framework versus being a distraction.

"Plan everything" is another of my golden rules. It is truly critical; without it, you cannot do your job correctly. It allows you to not just react to a situation when it becomes problematic, but rather to proactively avoid the problems in the first place via exposure through planning. I think your planning needs to go beyond the occasionally updated static project management of the past, and progress to online, dynamic digital dashboards. They can be driven via automated or regularly updated mechanisms, both systematic and manual. Because they can be constantly available, secure, and extremely detailed, you can actually use them to run your business or technology unit.

Another golden rule is "Be an open communicator." CTOs are highly visible, both externally and internally, so you have to understand how to state a vision, goal, or plan and socialize and evangelize it. These are all communication traits. Collaboration is essential; you have to be able to work well with others, whether they're external or internal to your company. It is very important to be able to hear what others are saying, what their desires are, what they need. They'll state business objectives constantly; if you're not listening, you won't deliver. If you are in a CTO role, you need to listen to the business objectives, ask the right questions to fully understand them, and maybe even steer a little bit if you think the objectives are going down an incorrect path.

"Desire to be in charge" is my final golden rule. A lot of responsibility comes with the CTO position. In most organizations, CTOs are part of the executive team, so being an executive – with the attendant communication and collaboration responsibilities – is also one of the roles a CTO fills. A desire to do the right thing for your company, using technology that will allow your company to be a success, should be a strong motivator for a CTO; otherwise, you shouldn't accept this type of very visible position.

You have to take joy out of your company's success and give up some of the "I" aspects of the success. As a CTO, if you have your eye on where the company is benefiting from technology, those you manage should notice and follow suit. You can eliminate some of the bickering that can go on in traditional business because you're focusing on something much broader than what you're personally doing; you're focusing on the overall success of your company.

The Technological Future

Convergence will finally happen. We will be able to interact with multiple media types in our daily lives through a variety of different mechanisms, whether it's broadband or wireless or some new ubiquitous access to content. That's very exciting and compelling to a CTO.

I've been fairly well connected, wired, for quite a while now. I began using two-way messaging when it first became available. I love the accessibility and my ability to interact with others and others to interact with me globally. I call instant messaging my virtual open door policy. When I'm online and available, my employees all over the world know I can be asked a question, no matter the time zone we're each in. I love being accessible, and the policy seems to be very beneficial, given the large, globally distributed teams I tend to lead. I love that I can be in one time zone, and I'm interacting with team members, no matter what time it is in another time zone, because that person needed to ask me a question.

I think that communicative capability will become much broader and better over time. It won't just be the pure technologists like me; it will be everyday people who are using it. In some regards, that breaks down a lot of cultural barriers. It breaks down regional and global boundaries, too. You can have a good friend living twelve time zones away, and the difference becomes totally irrelevant. They are available to interact and share their lives from opposite ends of the earth.

Common-sense use of technology will need to occur from an economic perspective. When the Internet bubble was occurring, we always thought of using the technology and taking a common-sense approach to it, realizing the bubble could burst very quickly, so we planned for the safe use of our technology and did not assume everything we touched would be turned to Internet gold. If you're thinking of investing in an application for your business, you're going to want something that you think is economical and will deliver cost-savings or generate revenue.

I've done a lot of due diligence on other companies as a CTO, and it's been amazing to realize during an analysis of a company that they had no concept of how much money they were spending on something that was critical to the success of their business. They hadn't judged it properly. That's not what a CTO's job is. A CTO's job is to ensure that you're putting in the right solution for the business objective and that it's costing you the right amount of money, not wasting money for the company. I think technology, in general, is going to have that rule to guide us: What is the business objective met by this technology, and will they together drive value for the company at large? The CTO is the right person to answer that question and own the implementation of the solution.

Michael Dunn was appointed to the position of chief technology officer, executive vice president, for Encoda Systems in June 2001 to oversee and coordinate technology development and implementation across all of Encoda's business units, addressing technology solutions for broadcasting, automation, advertising, cable, and Internet applications. Mr. Dunn has held senior positions with major companies in media and entertainment, broadcast, advertising, cable and Internet industries, most recently serving as corporate CTO for Time Warner Inc. While with Time Warner, he had both operational and strategic responsibilities, providing enterprise-wide leadership for technology research and development, architecture, infrastructure design, evaluating applications of new technologies, and setting standards. He was also the lead technologist for Time Warner Digital Media's Investment Fund, overseeing the technical due diligence of prospective companies.

Mr. Dunn started his career in development, moved into MIS/IT management, and has since spent most of the last ten years in CTO-type roles, where he has primarily focused on bridging business and technology objectives. Before Time Warner, he served as CTO of the online unit of Dell Computer Corporation. In that position, he had global leadership responsibility for Internet and Web technologies, investment governance, day-to-day site operations management, technical planning and architecture, partnerships, customer briefings, and future technology direction setting. Before joining Dell, Mr. Dunn held chief Internet and IT technologist positions at Americast, a closely held joint venture of Walt Disney Co. and several other companies that focused on broadband interactive TV and Internet access, and at True North Communications, a global advertising agency. Earlier in his career, he worked at Turner Broadcasting, where he was responsible for their technology efforts on the West Coast and in the Asia and Pacific regions.

Currently Mr. Dunn is involved as either a director or advisor on the boards of a number of companies, including QBeo, a Seattle-based developer of broadband digital imaging and video technologies and services; Internet Capital Group, a global B2B-focused company; Appgenesys, a Silicon Valley-based e-infrastructure management service provider focusing on complex Internet application deployment; and Zebware, a Silicon Alley-based Internet software development company focusing on next-generation dynamic Web toolsets. Mr. Dunn is the founding member of InfoWorld's CTO Advisory Council.

BRIDGING BUSINESS AND TECHNOLOGY: KEEPING THINGS AS SIMPLE AS POSSIBLE

MIKE RAGUNAS

StaplesDirect.com

Chief Technology Officer

The Role of the CTO

My role as CTO at StaplesDirect.com is to focus on developing and delivering e-commerce technologies in support of all of our different e-commerce ventures, including Staples.com, StaplesLink.com, Quill.com and BusinessDepot.com, our Canadian site. My focus is on how we deliver customer-facing and support technologies, and how to deliver them in a way that is best aligned with our business objectives.

I see myself as a bridge between our technology delivery capabilities and our business strategy. It is important to really understand both sides of that equation so that I can make sure we are delivering the technology that best matches our strategy. We add value to the business not just by building solutions, but by also bringing forward technologies and ideas that we think should be considered as part of the business strategy. I also partner across the business to help identify things that we can do to serve customers better.

I measure our IT organization on how much value we deliver to the business. We are here to help the business drive the top line and the bottom line – sales and profitability. For the last three and a half years since its inception, my team and I have been 100% focused on developing our Internet channel. Our success has been clear – we have built our e-commerce business from effectively zero in 1998 to what will be approaching a billion dollars in revenue in FY2001. The business has also begun to turn a profit for us, so we have achieved that rare feat in Internet business, to grow rapidly and deliver profitability at the same time.

Customers as Co-developers

We are in business to serve our customers. Never losing sight of this fact is a major driver in the technology we select. By serving our customers as best we can, we are able to maximize their value at Staples and make them more loyal customers. We don't just go out and develop a project based on what we think might work or if we think it is a "cool" technology. We are focused more on what we know about our customer, what we think they want, and how to understand better what they want. We, as a company, focus a lot of attention on gathering information about our customers, talking to them, testing things that we want to do with them, and making sure that those things are understandable and deliver value to them. We look to our customers to be co-developers with us. What we are delivering, from a technology perspective, is exactly what our customers need and want; things that they will use and will have the most benefit to the business overall.

Keeping it Simple

We have a general philosophy here to keep things as simple as possible. That manifests itself in terms of trying to minimize the number of different technologies we are using. This keeps our environment simpler. It also allows us to be much more flexible and nimble in flowing technology resources into areas where they are most needed. This allows us to deploy our technical talent more broadly across the board, rather than pigeonholing people into a particular technology space that is providing a narrow set of benefits to the company. We also look to select technologies that we believe have "legs," ones that we expect to be around and supported down the road. As a Fortune 500 company, we assess the long-term value of technology very carefully – when we put in a technology, we need it to scale and we expect it to last. We are growing very rapidly and have to make sure that things that we select today are going to meet the needs of the business several years down the road, not just today. That is sometimes difficult to do when you are growing rapidly in the dot-com space, where the technology is often immature. We are still using things that we built three years ago, but we have had to regularly update them to meet the changing current and future needs of the business.

It is easy to get caught up in looking for the most elegant technical solution for a problem, not realizing that the best technology may not provide the most value to the business. I believe in standardizing and picking technologies that may not be the most technically elegant, but that can be applied broadly to do multiple jobs well and that we know are going to have very strong vendor support down the road as well.

When we do a new project, we always look first at the technology we already have in house. Even though another technology may have a slightly higher degree of fit to our requirements, we will not bring in a new technology unless we have a compelling business case to offset the increased support and complexity costs of adding it in.

Being Technologically Nimble

Being technologically nimble means being able to respond quickly to new requirements and needs, and being able to support change on a rapid basis, even large scale changes. Being nimble involves both a philosophy of how you select, implement, and use technology, and how you manage your team of IT professionals behind it. Standardizing is important because we need to minimize the number of different technologies we have to manage. This links directly back to keeping things simple. As we build new things and put new systems in place, we work to do it in a modular way so that we allow ourselves the flexibility to change solutions more easily in the future.

Much of what we do is provide systems that support our customers and associates out in the field, as well as here at headquarters. One of the biggest challenges you have in a corporate environment in an enterprise like we have is integration of new things into your existing environment. We focus a lot of attention on how we can minimize the touch points between different applications, and make sure that we are able to bring in and out different pieces of the application at different points in time. From a technology perspective, a lot of our focus here is on how we can use middleware technology in between our applications to create a buffer that allows us more flexibility as we make changes around the business. Again, we always focus on simplicity, trying to keep things as simple as possible so that it is less complicated when you are faced with needing to make modifications. It is then easier to understand what is going on in the environment and identify places where you need to make changes and then implement those changes.

Staples has made a conscious effort as we've built out different parts of our business to refrain from building anything twice. If we already have something somewhere within the organization, we are going to try to leverage that as much as possible. A good example in our dot-com business is that we already had a delivery and catalog operation that had customer service and distribution fulfillment. Rather than going out and creating a separate instance of that for the dot-com part of our business, we built the dot-com part to be just a new order acceptance vehicle that could get orders into our existing customer service and distribution infrastructure. That has benefited us because we are able to then provide for our customers a single view of the company. When they call the Staples call center, they can ask about a catalog order they placed or a dot-com order they placed. We have also integrated the dot-com part of our business into our retail stores through in-store Internet Access Points (or kiosks), as a way to order products from our online inventory while in the stores. Again, rather than building something new to take an order in the store, we have adapted Staples.com to the store environment, leveraging the Staples.com infrastructure.

We focus on knitting all of our systems together into a common set of services to our customers across all of our different channels. Being nimble is a key part of implementing and further developing our multi-channel business to serve customers however they want to shop with Staples. This is our way of doing business now and in the future.

To Build or Buy

Building a custom solution versus buying a packaged solution is a question we deal with continually. Our bias is generally toward buying solutions where we can. In those cases, we are going to get the advantage of a vendor producing a solution for which the vendor can leverage their resources across a lot of different customers. If we built it ourselves, we would have to maintain the same kind of team that the vendor would have just to keep the application going. Where we think it is feasible, we are going to buy a solution and then modify it only where absolutely necessary. We particularly focus on buying packaged solutions for back office applications such as financials and human resources systems. These systems are critical to the operation of the company, but are not considered competitive differentiators.

Our approach will be different in places where we feel we have a strategic imperative. Some of our core customer-facing areas in particular, such as e-commerce, catalog order management, and retail point of sale, are where we are going to focus most of our in-house and custom development. These solutions are either fully custom or heavily modified packaged solutions. In the case of our e-commerce businesses, these are highly customized solutions because we feel it is important to offer exactly what our customers need, but also offer a differentiating experience with Staples that is really tapping into all that we have to offer within the company.

There is also another big question based on using internal resources for custom development versus using a third party. We base this decision on a number of factors. Do we have the appropriate skill sets internally? If we do, are those resources available, or are they committed to another project? Are there other benefits we can get from using a third party? When we first built a number of our e-commerce businesses, we did much of the work with third parties, but always kept our team plugged into the development process so we could pick up the application once it was completed. At the same time, we were building our own internal team to do follow-on releases and development of those products. In general, we are only going to bring in third parties for custom development when we have a need for the particular skill or when we have a project that we don't have the resources internally to do ourselves. In those cases, we either outsource the project entirely, or we put together a joint team of our resources and a third party resource to develop something.

Executing Technology Projects

One of our key areas of focus is predictably delivering the value that we need to deliver to the business. One of the general challenges around technology projects is figuring out how to make sure that you will get them done on time and delivering the value that was expected. We focus very heavily on the project management process within technology projects. All of our major projects have assigned project managers who work very closely with our counterparts in the business to define exactly what it is we are trying to do and make sure we are all clear about what we are expecting to deliver. We also make sure that we keep the deliverables organized into manageable blocks that have fairly short timelines associated with them. We generally don't do long term projects in which you don't get anything until the end of the project. We are very focused on figuring out what we can do in a matter of weeks or months to deliver some initial value and then build upon that with follow-on releases to continue adding incremental value. With all of our e-commerce properties, we are very focused on defining clear and manageable sets of functionality that we can deliver, focusing on the ones that have the highest business value and doing them in a way that allows us to deliver that value in a short period of time and then move on to the next deliverable.

For us, serving customers comes down to looking at how our customers want to interact with us, and how we can offer those things in a way that provides the best shopping experience for customers. For example, in our e-commerce businesses, we offer a variety of ways in which you can interact with us. You can work with us over the phone, over email, or even through a live chat solution right from the website. In all of those cases, you are dealing with the same set of call center associates who are servicing phone, fax, and other ordering channels. These associates therefore have access to all of your orders and can help you with any question. Technology enables us to provide customers different avenues to shop with us, and then letting the customer choose which way is more convenient and appropriate for them. We don't push one over the other. Some companies will hide their 800 numbers because they would rather have someone send them an email. We put our number right out there on every page of our website, but we also put icons to email us or chat with us, because some people might prefer to use those mechanisms. We track very closely our handling on all of those things. We make sure we are providing response levels to all those different channels that our customers would expect.

I look at my team as having customers directly, as well, such as our internal customers with whom we partner to bring these things to the market. It is very important to think about what we do in the technology space as providing a service for our own customers, and it is very important that we live up to their expectations, because like anything else, it is very easy for a customer to lose confidence in you if you are unreliable. From our perspective, "delivering reliably" is extremely important because it allows us to be partners in building the business and delivering that value, but to also make sure that the business can count on getting the value that we are expected to deliver at the time it is needed. We can then bake those benefits into our business plans and use them to drive profitability and sales in the business.

We are also very focused on managing and communicating expectations for our team. For example, we publish a scorecard weekly that tells all the people around our business how we are doing on delivering the projects that they are expecting. So we can tell them very quickly whether we are on track or not, what we are planning to spend, and when we are planning to deliver these things. We do that for every single project we have that has any kind of expectation set. We make sure that everyone is one hundred percent aware of what we are doing and how we are doing, and then we measure our entire team on how well they deliver against those expectations. We also distribute the scorecard to everyone on my team, so they know how they are doing as well and what we are telling the business about their projects.

Focus on Strategy, Not Technology

The CTO's focus should be at least as much on the fit of the technology organization and strategy to the business as it is on the fit of the technology itself. There are lots of good technologies out there, and there are many technical solutions that will work equally well to solve any given business problem. It is unusual to find a company where the technology they have cannot meet the needs of the business, from a pure platform perspective. What is more important is understanding the alignment of the technology organization with the goals of the business and how well they are using the technology they have. You will run into more issues from a lack of alignment of IS or IT objectives with the real strategies and objectives of the business, and a lack of partnership between technology and business, than you will from people implementing technology that is just not going to work.

In assessing an IT shop, it is easy to figure out what technologies are being used and where they are being used. It takes more time to get a sense of whether the organization is aligned well. It also takes longer to understand whether the applications in place have been developed with a view toward supporting the future needs of the business. You must look at how the applications were developed, how they were architected, and how they are set up to allow for and support change in the business, as opposed to dealing with a particular need at a point in time.

The Future of Technology

As technology is getting more complex, it is also getting more intelligent. One of the trends that I have seen is that technology professionals are spending less and less of their time actually coding technology, assembling the bits and bytes. They are spending more of their time configuring and implementing technology in direct support of business needs. Successful technologists must become more and more business experts and understand how to deploy technology in support of business objectives. They need to be less focused on knowing a particular bit of technology. Technology changes so rapidly that we need to be flexible in what technology we use to solve a business problem. The days when a programmer could spend an entire career working with one programming language are over. What is going to be most valuable and get to be more so going forward is people who understand how technology provides value and can understand the needs of a business and be able to figure out the right technology to put in place, and how to do it most effectively.

We look at all of our technology decisions in the context of our customers. We try to avoid jumping on technology bandwagons. An example is wireless. We look at wireless connectivity to our customers as an example of something that we just don't see a great driving need for in our business right now. A lot of companies went out and spent a lot of money on building wireless interfaces into their business, and nothing came of it. In our case, we are going to really focus on the things that might not be as glamorous, but things that will move the lever in our business, which is based on understanding what our customers are really going to use and need.

The future of technology must increasingly consider the people interfacing with it – customers. Our company focuses across our business on usability. This takes the form of talking to our customers, understanding how they think about things and interact with us, and making sure that the things that we bring to market are things that we are going to get the full value out of because we have usability tested them. We are using that concept across our business now and doing usability work on internal applications that just work with our own associates. We recognize that in a company like ours, with 50,000 associates, we can't afford to go out there and train all of them on how to use an application. It has to be intuitive. It has to be something that people can understand just by looking at it, and it also has to be able to conform to common standards about how people interact with technology. It is best when people can pick something up and understand it right away. That concept applies with our external customers as well as internally with our associates. Our key drivers are really focusing on technology as very easy to use and enabling tremendous value in the businesses.

Golden Rules of Being a CTO

One of the key rules as a CTO is to understand at least as much about your business as you do about technology. You need to be clear about what your business is there to do and how you, as CTO, can support and help drive the success of that business. Particularly at the CTO level, it is important that you spend as much time learning about your business as you do technology. Having achieved CTO level, you probably know enough about technology already; however, you may not know enough about your customers or your business to maximize your ability to contribute.

Don't assume that you personally represent your typical customer. If you are developing technology for non-technical customers, you are most likely not going to be able to think like your customers. Your products must be developed with your customers' needs in mind, not your own. We rely very heavily on usability experts in the design and development of our products. You have to understand how your customers are going to interact with your products and not allow your own biases as a technologist to come into play when you are developing a product that is going to meet a customer need.

Keep things simple. Try to minimize complexity. No matter what you do, you will end up with an environment that is more complex than you would like; whatever you can do to keep it simpler is always going to put you in a better position to be nimble. Don't deploy a new technology without a strong business case to support it. Every technology you add to your environment will add complexity and support costs; make sure it's worth it.

Make sure your team is working on the things that have the most value. As a business grows, there is a tendency for that focus to get diffused sometimes. I make sure that my team works very closely with the key leaders in our business to identify the things that have the most impact, and to make sure that we are focusing as many of our resources as possible on those things. We pick a small number of key initiatives that we focus on "nailing," and then deliver those things on time with everything that was planned in order to make sure that we get the full business benefit of the original idea.

Another big focus for me is building the team, getting the right people on the team, hiring well, and making sure that the team has the right support and training to do the things that we ask them to do. We have to make sure we have the right team and that they have the right capabilities and equipment to deliver maximum value consistently.

The Holy Grail of Technology

I have always been fascinated by the "replicator" in Star Trek, which is the device that fabricates anything you ask it to make, seemingly from thin air. Today the field of nanotechnology is focused on developing this same type of solution, in which materials can be manipulated at the molecular level to make microscopic machines, or to produce larger objects molecule by molecule. I am by no means an expert in this field, but the potential applications of this technology – both good and bad – are mind-boggling. It is fascinating to think about what would change in the world if everyone had a machine that could make anything.

Mike heads development and implementation of e-commerce and related technologies for Staples.com, the e-commerce business of Staples, Inc., the $11 billion retailer of office supplies, business services, furniture and technology. A 15-year veteran of Staples, Mr. Ragunas was formerly director of strategic technology and systems architecture for the company, where he managed the selection and use of leading-edge technologies and led the initial development of Staples.com. He was recently named one of InfoWorld magazine's Top 25 Most Influential CTOs. Mr. Ragunas is a graduate of Harvard University.

THE ART OF BEING A CTO – FOSTERING CHANGE

RICK BERGQUIST

PeopleSoft

Chief Technology Officer

The Role of the CTO

The responsibilities of the CTO vary widely from company to company because of the varying needs of each organization. At PeopleSoft, the role is for an individual who understands technology and how it can be applied for business solutions, and then sees that it gets applied or convinces people that the company has to change to use the new technology going forward. It requires an understanding of technology, an understanding of what is possible, and an understanding of the business, because, at the end of the day, we're driving forward to make businesses successful and to fit into that whole strategy.

My job is to consume vast amounts of data and distill it down to manageable amounts. It's a job for which there are no shortcuts. You're always looking for that one nugget of information to give you insight into a new way of doing things.

Success, Leadership and Teams

You must have the ability to avoid getting stuck in time. You have to be able to envision the possibility of the way things could be. The key to success is a willingness to change; otherwise, you are just reinventing the old wheel. On the other hand, you must have grounding in the principles of your organization – you have to know what makes your business successful, and you have to reinforce those things. You have the freedom to do things differently, but know that what you do differently should be aligned with the organization's values. If you can't align with the organization, either you will tear it down, or it will resist the change.

To be a leader, you have to make the right analysis and fight for the right thing. Leaders in technology understand how something could be different; then they work to make it so. Sometimes it just takes persistence to get things done. In the end, it is the ability to say, "Let's make this place better," that creates the change. Then, if your track record is good, people will believe you the next time around.

I think I am successful because successful people surround me. I have the opportunity to represent thousands of developers at PeopleSoft. It's all about us working together.

To be successful, you need good communication skills, so you can articulate your ideas. You have to be a sharp listener to pick up the nuggets of information you get from the people around you.

It is also important how you relate to and seek out diverse opinions. Dysfunctional organizations often have a running feud between the sales and product staff. As CTO, you have to bridge these groups by putting yourself in sales' shoes to understand what they are trying to do and how they hope to overcome obstacles. You have to ask yourself what the salespeople are complaining about. Is it a product deficiency, or is it that they do not understand how to position the value of what you are offering? What does the sales force see on the front lines that your developers do not see? You have to have the ability to transcend your own job role to understand someone else's point of view. You have to break down these barriers to be effective.

I think you need to understand enough technology to appreciate the different pieces and how they all work together, and then synthesize them to the essence of what this new technology can give you. You have to understand what it has now and what it had before. Then you have to have the ability to apply that toward your business. That leads then to convincing and working with other people to affect change. When you combine all of those things, I think you will be successful.

Common Threads of Technology

Technology enables you to do things differently.

Let's take the Internet. We're out of the hype of the Internet bubble, which claimed, "Everything about your business has changed." Some things haven't changed – commercial enterprises still care about revenue and profit. Those that didn't are out of business.

What has changed fundamentally? The Internet was and continues to be a profound technology whose potential is just beginning to be realized.

To see how our company has harnessed the changes in technology through time, let's look at our own technology as a case study.

As a startup, PeopleSoft envisioned two things:

Simplified User Interface

Client/server systems could make a vast improvement in the user interface – the prior generation of systems was mainframe systems that used a character-based 3270 display. The whole interface revolved around code values that required operators to undergo long periods of training to master. Navigation revolved around memorizing "transaction codes" to move from one screen to another. With the emergence of the Windows environment, we saw the possibility of deploying systems that could use menus to allow for simple application navigation, and the Windows user interface that no longer relied on code values, but rather let users interact with the system, naturally selecting options without requiring codes. This great user interface enabled many more people to interact with systems without having to attend extensive training classes to learn arcane navigation techniques and memorize code values. Mere mortals could now use applications.

Quickly Adaptable Systems

Mainframe systems were unable to adapt to business changes quickly. They had been built using large amounts of COBOL code that was inflexible and unable to adapt to change. Every IT organization had an infinite backlog of system change requests. With a quickly adaptable system, you could make changes at the speed of business changes – your applications became business enablers instead of being boat anchors holding you back.

Recognizing the two fundamental benefits that the new client/server technology could solve provided the basis for the products that our company produced. It was this technology that enabled our company to become a successful startup company and mature into a billion dollar organization.

Yet, when the times change, you have to be prepared to walk away from what made you successful. In our case, the client/server technology we pioneered was just an enabler to create business applications that enabled our customers to run their organizations more efficiently and effectively. The client/server applications were our roots – they were our legacy. But if we hadn't been prepared to move on, they also would have been our demise.

We recognized that a new paradigm was being created by the emergence of the Internet. It was a technology that enabled a universal method of accessing business systems – available to all employees, all customers, all partners, and all suppliers. And best of all, it was a technology that was ubiquitously deployed – it didn't require anyone to install applications for their use. This technology would allow us to create whole new business solutions that could be deployed to a much wider audience than we had reached before.

Yet this was a risky adventure: We had to be prepared to say that all of our applications were obsolete – that they all needed to be replaced. We had to convince the naysayers in our own organization that the new world was going to be a better place. We had to answer such queries as, "We've been working on this technology for 12 years and have perfected it. Why are we moving to an unproven model that puts our applications on the Web – a technology known for intermittent performance and questionable security?"

Working with the visionaries within our organization, we were able to tackle these objections one by one – to prove the technology could stand up.

We tackled security by showing how the new Internet technologies could replace existing technologies. Encryption provided by the browser was used to protect confidential data. Directory servers allowed the users to have single-sign-on capabilities enabling them to have one user ID and password to access all systems. This improved security because users had only one password, which they could memorize and not have to write down. This reduced costs because IT had only one repository to maintain, not dozens.

With respect to performance, scalability, and reliability, we saw the future as being the deployment of not only hundreds of internal users, as client/server systems had been, but thousands of partners or suppliers, and tens of thousands of customers. We tackled performance

145

and reliability through a server architecture that was efficient. As user demand increased, you simply added hardware to match it. Reliability was provided by having redundant servers that could take over when any other server failed.

We revisited the whole user experience and realized we had two choices: The cheapest one was to simply port the Windows look, feel, and functionality over to the Web. Or we could reengineer the user experience to match the Web metaphor. We choose the second alternative. We reasoned that the value of the Web was our ability to deploy our applications out to everyone – every employee, every partner, every supplier, and every customer. To deploy universally meant that the user experience had to be intuitive to users whose everyday experience was the Web. Applications had to require no formal training courses. This meant a complete rewrite of the applications to be pure Internet applications, not "Windows on the Web," like some of our competitors.

Our company spent $500 million to make these fundamental changes to our technology. We raised our R&D spending to 27 percent of our revenues in an arena where our peers spend 8 percent to 15 percent on R&D. What enabled us to be bold enough to bet the company on this strategy? This action came about because all the organizations within the company got behind it: The sales organization saw the competition as the emerging startups that were Web-based; the product strategists saw this as an enabler to change basic business processes with ubiquitous access; our customers saw the possibilities for lower costs because supporting a browser was 90 percent cheaper than installing code on a client.

Ultimately we had a good understanding of our mission as a company. History shows that companies that don't really understand their business miss evolving as technology changes. For example, the railroad companies thought of themselves as railroads and didn't realize they should have been thinking of themselves as transportation companies. They missed out on these possibilities and didn't transform their business. At our company we realize we are in the business of delivering technology-enabled business solutions – we are not a client/server company. We also learned from history – none of the vendors that were predominant in the mainframe era made it into the client/server era. They didn't have the will to change. The new way to do business solutions in the new world was to do it on the Internet, and we had to get there.

Maintaining a technology lead is the delicate balance of establishing how the technology can change your business and having the vision and will to completely transform current practices. This requires working with all of the parts of your organization and crafting a common vision of the future.

A CTO's most obvious sign of success is keeping his or her job. The criteria involve asking basic questions: Are we staying current with technology? Are we perceived as a leader with our product and our technology? Are we moving forward, or are we becoming a legacy player? Are we working more efficiently? Do we have better products that meet the needs of our customers? Are we enabling people to thrive in business with the technology that exists today?

Changes in Technology

The Internet is the broad new wave of technology, and we're just at the start of a ten-year cycle. The Internet has changed our ability to communicate and interact with people. We're just beginning to understand how that will change business processes and the interaction between companies and their customers. There is a very bright future ahead. You can do things differently, but it's a freeing experience. It's scary for some people, but it's a good thing.

Our pure Internet architecture has given us a 24-month lead over our competitors. Client/server lasted about ten years, and its major features were effectively limited to a better user interface and the ability to adapt faster. We saw the potential of the Internet as even broader:

1.   The Internet lowers the cost of doing business by reducing the cost of deploying applications. It is a lot cheaper to deploy systems over a browser than to install code on client.

2.   The Internet provides universal access to business that enables organizations to work collaboratively with their customers,

partners, and suppliers. The most profound change of the Internet is that we now have an environment where clients, partners, and suppliers all have the same infrastructure to access systems as easily as consumers can access anything over their browsers, such as Yahoo! or Amazon. Businesses have the ability to change business processes and have access to information they never had before. Customers can place orders for products and report problems using self-service features. You can provide your partners with leads, and they can track them down.

A common problem for many businesses was that with channel partners to sell their products, there was little visibility into potential problems. The ability to expand the access to systems via the Internet can help run a more efficient business because it gives the decision-makers insight into what is really going on. Businesses are changing their processes. The Internet is the enabler for it. A simple example is FedEx. They gave you the ability to access their Web site to find out where your package is. For you it's a benefit. You can do it yourself. You don't have to worry about someone entering the number incorrectly. FedEx cut their costs dramatically by not having a staff call center. This is an example of a win-win, where the business process changed to give both parties better information on a timely basis and reduced costs. We're just beginning to see how processes can be changed to do this. It really does follow the macro trend. Companies no longer try to do everything themselves. Vertical integration went out with Henry Ford. You're now using partners or outsourcing, or you're doing virtual organizations that are doing things. But to be effective in those virtual organizations, you have to have access to the core information so people can make informed decisions so you don't lose things during translation. That's what the Internet enables products to give you. You can deploy the applications in a universal scheme.

Business processes are being enabled as Web services to reduce the cost of setting up collaboration. The drive for universal access is being aided by the development of standards to allow business process to be seen as a set of services that can be more easily accessed than the stiff interfaces that have been present in the past.

New devices are emerging; the reign of the PC as the dominant device for accessing the Internet is declining. Mobile workers want mobile access, whether it's by taking their data with them or accessing it via wireless technologies. People are demanding access to information from more convenient devices, such as PDAs and phones. These new types of devices will form an adjunct to the PC of today and will allow access instantly. By removing the barriers to information systems, a whole new class of users can be served, and their work can be made more effective.

Privacy Issues

The first problem we have with privacy is the definition – we don't have a full understanding of what it means and what we're trying to achieve. On one hand, we say we don't want anyone to have too much access to our personal information. The problem is if you want a promotion in a corporation, you want every one of the higher managers to know about you and everything you have accomplished. In this case, you want fairly wide dissemination of data. What you have to understand about privacy is that you must ascertain whether you want certain people to see your data and what you want them to see. You have to establish the criteria. The real issue is often reaching a common understanding of what we are protecting and from whom.

Technologically, I found I can protect any of the information using pieces of it, but the challenge is to ask yourself, "What is the end goal?" There are times when we want a wide dissemination of data and other times when we don't. For instance, in marketing, if you disseminate information about your likes and dislikes, then companies can actually get rid of a lot of junk mail to you because they'll realize that you're not going to buy anything anyway. Do you see that as a positive or a negative? Do you want to sort through all the junk mail? The material is a lot more targeted to you. I think the challenge that society has to face is finding out what the mix is between those two, so that information can be used by both parties, but it doesn't get abused by either one.

Challenges

The biggest challenge I face is getting people to think about what could be, as opposed to what is. People like to continuously fine-tune the way things are. Enacting change is one of the hardest things to do. Machiavelli pointed out that change is the hardest thing to bring about because people always have a vested interest in the way things are.

If you have an organization that is used to change and that embraces the concept of change, then you're going to make changes for good business decisions. You have to be an evangelist. You have to identify the problems, enumerate them, and then identify the vision to make it better. Businesses can evangelize about making more money by solving the customers' needs.

Staying Technologically Nimble

In the proliferation of technologies that are emerging today, the key question for a CTO is, "What is just cool as opposed to what is profound?" I generally try to solve this riddle by envisioning the effects of the new technology. Will this reduce the cost of applications? Will it reduce the cost of doing business? Does it enable companies to do business in a completely different way? There have been many things I thought were really cool, but in the end, I don't know how well they would have been accepted and don't know how they would have changed everyone else's life (remember PointCast?). In the end, you can't stand behind technology if it's not growing the business or cutting costs. You just have to let those cool things go by. Maybe some other day you can envision it a different way, but if it doesn't meet the test of transforming or growing the business, or reducing costs, then it's just an interesting anomaly along the way.

To be successful both individually and as an organization, I think you have to have a vast appetite for taking in information. You then have to have the ability to dissect it and separate the good ideas from the ones that are just curiously interesting. You have to be open to a variety of sources. I haven't found one single source that I could read and say, "I've found everything I need."

Information comes from a multitude of sources. It can come from your customers and from fellow employees. It certainly comes from the media who expose what other companies are doing. You get leading-edge ideas from professors who are writing books. You get information from all of these different sources, and the challenge is to turn that raw data into information that's relative to your organization. You depend on people to synthesize that information and bring it together into a vision of where you're taking your company. Each individual has to figure out what sources to deal with to make himself more effective in his individual job. Each organization has to have in place a culture that is accepting and thriving on change.

We want to make sure we're current with technology to enable us to do business differently. That's why an organization has to have a culture. Those will be the thriving organizations that tolerate change, change the rules, and promote people for bringing out new ways of doing things. In some ways it runs counter-intuitive to the order of the world, where people like things to be steady. People say, "I'm all for progress, as long as you don't change anything I have to deal with." You have to have a culture where, once in a while, things are done differently. What you have to promote is not change for change's sake, but change for the business' sake.

Companies are better suited for change when they have a culture that thrives on information interchange. Look at the things you've hoarded. If they were gold, you'd have a whole stockpile of gold, and then you'd be rich. This attitude has pervaded the thinking that information is something that should be hoarded. The cultural change that companies have to realize is that information is not what's valuable – it's the exchanging of information. It's what people do with the information that's actually more valuable than the information itself.

The most effective organizations think about interchange of information among the people in the organization. They think about being willing to share it with your partners and suppliers and others. Even if there's a risk of information getting out to a competitor, an organization that can share and act on information quickly often has an advantage. It's what you do with information that has value in today's economy. That's the cultural change that will determine the ultimate winners from the losers.

Building a Team

Execution from a technology standpoint is really no different from any other endeavor. First, you have to agree on the vision – the goal you're going to achieve. Then you have to build a plan to achieve the goal. It has been said that the difference between a hallucination and a vision is the presence of a viable plan to achieve the vision. You have a process for identifying the goals of your organization, although the way to go about this is not always clear, as the means that each organization uses are diverse and often subject to personalities and company practice. But no matter the process, the common thread will be the ability to lay out what can be and why it is in the organization's interest to do it.

The process is no different from everything else. It's a project management execution strategy, where you lay out the goals, the milestones, and the steps you need to accomplish those milestones and the resources you need. Then you have to have the diligence to monitor and control those elements.

Ultimately though, I've always found the most important resource is your people. No significant endeavor ever gets done by one person – you need to build a team that comprises people with the right skills to accomplish the goals. Recognize that not all people are experts at everything. You need to match your people with the skills that are required. Some of the best execution people have no vision. Some of the people who have vision have no execution skills. Think of it as a football team. A successful football team will have a great quarterback, a great line, receivers, and so forth. But you wouldn't expect the quarterback to be on the defensive line. Identify those skill sets required to execute the project. Make sure you have the right alignment to achieve the project goals.

Goals

Setting goals is definitely important, and you can measure progress against them by product release cycles and penetration of your product in the marketplace. This is important because without measurements toward goals, it's all practice.

The challenge in many places is that people have always had calendar cycles – quarterly or yearly planning. Technology doesn't move according to those cycles. You have to set up goals that match your fiscal calendar, but then you have to be willing to change the goals if the ground rules change, or the marketplace or economy has changed. If you're smart, you'll recognize when an external occurrence has changed and invalidated the plans you have made. Then you set up new goals.

Be aware of the external factors you counted on, and as soon as they change, reexamine your premises. Prepare a new set of goals. Don't just march down the same path. Make new plans and new MBOs when it's appropriate.

Taking Risks

A risk to me means you're willing to try new things that can be accomplished in new ways. A lot of questions emerge when you're envisioning what could be. Will this work? We may not be smart enough to see the unintended consequences of things. You need to take risks in an organization; if you don't take risks, then you won't move forward.

There is definitely an advantage in being the first one with a new product or a new technology. You reap the rewards before anyone can catch up. You have to try a number of things. You have to pick your risks wisely. You have to "go boldly where no man has gone before," and if it's a morass, you have to deal with it. It's a tradeoff, like everything else.

We generally look at risk from a business case perspective. We look for what it's going to cost so we can foresee the consequences if we fail. We see risk in different things. In some places, you take low-risk ventures, and in others, you might take high risk, but you don't bet the whole company. There were times when our company took a risk on the Internet. In essence, it was about the company approach. We knew if we weren't on that new wave, then we wouldn't be in business. You have to size up each of the risks. What are the risks of doing something? What are the risks of not doing something? Often the risk of not doing something is greater than the risk of moving forward.

You have to be willing to express your opinions on those issues. You pick the things that make big changes, and you become a proponent. I think you have to be able early on to build a set of allies who say, "This is how we can complement what you're trying to do." You're really trying to make the whole organization successful. I think when we work it from that perspective, then people will help you deal with things. You must be working toward a shared goal.

Selling Your Vision

There are many different ways to sell a vision. One way is articulating your vision to people to see if it resonates. A corporation is not just technologists. You have to interact with the other parts, as an engine has to hit on all the cylinders to run well.

If I have an idea for the way things should be, then I go to the sales organization and see if they can sell it. I'll talk to our customer base to see if this meets a pain point they have and if it would solve the problem. I'll talk to our support people to see if this will solve a problem where they're hoping someone will have a solution. You can't just sell your vision on a technology basis. It has to meet the needs of the market and show that it will be good for your organization as a whole.

Interacting With Other Groups

My belief is that you often learn a lot just by being around the water cooler, listening to problems other people have or hearing about innovations they've done that no one else has thought of. Part of what you want to do is connect the right people who are doing similar things. The role of a management team is to foster innovation by connecting people. It's my belief that, in the end, organizations don't do anything – people do. So if you get the right people, you'll be amazed at what you can accomplish.

Our sales organization has early insights into what prospects are looking for because everyone who goes out to buy a product has visions of what they're trying to solve. You'll get a different set of insights from your customers because they're not really focused on the future, but on taking what they have and getting it to work really well.

Managing During Turbulent Markets

Our Company has a set of traditional values – we always believe revenues and profits count. Those values align us with the values of our customers – we're making them more successful, more profitable, and able to grow their organizations. These principles count, whether the marketplace is expanding or contracting. What does change is the focus.

In an expanding market where the focus is growth, companies must decide how to grow at a rapid rate. In a more challenging or declining market, the question is how to cut costs to survive. Both of those are present in all the solutions we deal with. We are an organization that's aimed at profit, and to get that profit, we have to provide a superior solution that people are willing to pay us for. It's understanding the customers' level of pain and how we can make their lives easier.

Best Skills

The ability to learn and do new things and change are the best skills to have. Everything we do in technology has a very short shelf life. I can look at my career and see that. The languages have all changed since the beginning of my career, and they'll change again. If you have the ability to surf the waves of change, you'll do well. You need to have the ability to be good at something, to learn it fast and to understand what's different about it and make use of it. Don't get so stuck on it that you miss the next big thing that's there. It's a skill of lifelong learning. It'll keep you fresh, and it will keep you challenged. I think you need all of those things to be effective in your job.

Be prepared to change and be prepared to foster change. There's the old prayer asking to let me change the things I can, accept the things I can't

155

change, and know the difference. I think that's what the CTO role implies. You're not there just to identify with the status quo. You're not there as a caretaker for what is. You're expected to ask where it can be.

The rules for technology will change, too. What's cool today will be passé in a few years. Like everything else, if you wait around for the future, you won't accomplish anything. Find out the best alternative today; make use of it; and when there's something better, change your goal and switch.

Best Advice

My first boss, John Grillos, said, "Pick your battles." The criteria for picking them are straightforward:

They have to be important.
They have to be winnable.
They have to be few.

We all have more opportunities to change things or to take on different battles, but you have to know how to choose them. You don't want to be fighting all the time; otherwise, nobody will want to deal with you. Pick things that are important because they will have the longest-lasting effect. Avoid causes that can't be won to conserve your resources for things you can change. If you can examine the battles facing you by these criteria, you generally come out ahead.

Whatever you do, enjoy it. You're going to spend a great majority of your life working at it. Most of us don't have jobs you leave behind – it doesn't end when you walk out the office door. You think about it later, even if you're home. If you enjoy what you're doing, and you're in the backyard thinking about it, that's fun. If you don't enjoy your job, go find another one.

Dream Technology

My goal is to make sure that every day we are working toward the dream technology. At our company, that technology is to make organizations run more effectively. To enable this, we need to make people more effective. When we get this right, the technology will fade into the background but be ever present. The technology will capture data at its source without anyone thinking about it.

Business processes will flow seamlessly across customers, partners, and suppliers. Information will be available for people to do their jobs effectively through intuitive interfaces. And change will be accommodated quickly. Systems will automatically suggest changes to optimize the business, based on continuous monitoring. Alternatively, people will be able to call up information easily to enable them to use their own creativity to foster change. I see a symbiotic world where the judgment, creativity, and innovation of people are matched with the speed, accuracy, and predictability of computers.

Rick Bergquist, senior vice president, chief technology officer, Technology and Applications Strategy, is responsible for PeopleSoft's long-term technology vision. In this position, he is responsible for identifying new technologies for deployment within PeopleSoft products in areas such as the Internet, data warehousing, knowledge management, and object-oriented technology.

At PeopleSoft, Mr. Bergquist was one of the original PeopleTools developers and has previously managed the PeopleTools development and strategy teams.

Before joining PeopleSoft, Mr. Bergquist was with American Management Systems, Inc., most recently as a senior principal in the product development group. While at AMS, he supervised the development of the company's application packages for retail banking.

Mr. Bergquist completed the Program for Management Development at the Harvard School of Business, and he holds a bachelor's degree in computer science from California Polytechnic State University.

DEVELOPING BEST OF BREED TECHNOLOGIES AND CAPABILITIES

DR. DAVID WHELAN

Boeing, Space and Communications

Chief Technology Officer

The CTO as Chief Innovation Officer

The role of the CTO varies from company to company. In fact, in each industry you see a different use of the CTO. At our company, we consider the position more of a chief innovation officer. This CTO role nurtures and cultivates new ideas and innovation in both the technologies and the processes by which we build and design large complex aerospace systems. These new systems include the Global Positioning System, which we were instrumental in developing and which can enable new military and civilian capabilities for our country.

The CTO must focus the enterprise or company so it can be responsive to new technology and capitalize on it. The CTO tries to organize the enterprise to focus and develop technology and capabilities, so we can offer our customers the "best of breed" in people and the best solutions to their problems. We must find the best processes and technology that facilitate optimal performance at minimal cost for our customers and products.

Internally, I try to challenge the technologists in the company to strive for excellence and help in recruiting the best talent needed in the various areas of expertise within the company. A large aerospace systems company such as ours needs expertise across a large domain of technologies, ranging from software to microelectronics design, to aircraft aerodynamics design, to propulsion systems, rocketry, and navigation. In essence, our needs run the gamut in technologies, and as such, we need the specialists across that entire spectrum. We continually strive to maintain our world-class strength and performance in these areas. We frequently ask the question, "In which areas do we need to excel?" And in turn, we focus on those key areas. It is virtually impossible to be the best in every area, so you have to strategize where you want to focus your energies and invest your resources and strengths. We also like to determine where it is possible to leverage other people's investments – investments in both people and in resources.

To me, the success of the CTO is really measured by gauging the health of the company. Every company must strive for continuous growth; it is the only way for a company to flourish in today's marketplace. You cannot allow a company to stagnate. If you do, the market will undervalue your potential, and you will become prey to market forces. You really must have a growth strategy, one based on both technology evolution and market expansion.

At our company, growth is about new technologies, new products, and the creation of new markets enabled by those new technologies. New technologies can be introduced to existing markets with relatively low risk, and conversely, new markets can be developed leveraging existing technology, also with low risk. We have examples of both of these growth approaches in the development of our new Global Air Traffic Management (ATM) business and in the ConneXion by Boeing™ in-flight commercial aircraft networking business. Most interesting, though, is our attention to the new technology and new market creation opportunities. These represent the highest risk, but also yield high payoff – we think of them as enabled by the emergence of new and disruptive technologies. These disruptive technologies usually render an existing market and technology obsolete with a new and larger market that can be addressed only with a new technical approach. So it is this interplay of the two that really creates the exciting opportunities for growth.

In terms of concerns or threats, as a CTO, the one thing you always have to worry about is technological surprise. A CTO must understand how technology is evolving and, likewise, how the marketplaces are evolving. A company must know it isn't prudent to ride a technology horse too long or in a fashion with blinders on, so you can't see a new idea or technology coming along. You must be adaptive so you can change technologies and be responsive to the marketplace.

Finally, you must also maintain a healthy workforce in terms of the technical depth of the company. You need a good, strong team of technologists and innovators that will catapult your company to a world-class organization in both creating technologies and creating solutions to the customers' problems. It is important that you do not allow your enterprise, from the technology point of view, to become slow, inefficient or expensive. Those are the three prescriptions for the death of an enterprise. The CTO must ensure that the "slide in technical performance" doesn't creep up on an organization and overwhelm it.

Right Technologies, Nimble Technologies

Deciding on the right technologies is about having a healthy enough depth of talent across an enterprise to be aware of your customers' needs and challenges and to be aware of technology and its evolution. It's about having the proper balance between technology's push and customer requirements' pull, meaning the customer's demand for new solutions to problems. So I like to work with my people to inspire them, to set the course for them in terms of the new technological directions. I want to give them the resources to allow them to innovate, invent, and create new solutions. It is that kind of enterprise you are trying to create, so that from a technology point of view, the organization is world-class. As a famous rock star once said, "I may not be whom they are cheering for, but I am the cheerleader."

In terms of keeping the company technologically nimble, a physics professor once told me, "Physics is not a spectator sport." In other words, you have to be involved. You have to be doing the work for yourself. You have to be on the front line, driving the innovation, creating the new product, generating the new ideas. Only then can you set the course, create new solutions, and be the first to market and dominant in your market area. As you look at the technologies, you need to choose your mix of the various strategies across the different technology areas and the balance that best allows your enterprise to be adaptable to change, both in terms of matching your people strength and matching your customer needs.

In our view, we are creating a new class of enterprise that is a "network-centric organization," an enterprise that allows information to flow throughout the organization, giving complete transparency of decision and action. Being an aware, adaptive organization that understands technology and understands its customer's needs is what adapting to change is about, and we believe a network-centric organization is the key to achieving those results.

The Future of Technology

Let me take the limits off the horizons and speak to some of the natural trends I think are important to our company as an enterprise and, by association, probably important to a lot of different enterprises. My view is that we are still in the midst of the transistor revolution that began in the 1950s. We have continued to force maturation and exponentiation of the technology to the point where I believe that by next year, we will be able to put a billion transistors on the chip.

Having done this, we will have moved from the age of microelectronics to the age of nanoelectronics. In those 50 years, we have seen the size of electronics continue to shrink, the complexity continue to increase, the cost continue to decrease, the speed continue to increase, and the energy consumed by the electronics continue to improve. All these benefits roll up into our ability to do more and more with less and less, both in terms of volume and weight, but potentially even more important in terms of power consumed by the electronics. And that enables us to do things you would have not dreamed possible 20 years ago. Think of the global satellite communication systems available to us – we can provide voice and data communications to any part of the world.

We now have very sophisticated instruments for understanding materials and processes that allow us to build new materials that we never dreamed possible, such as bandgap engineered materials and carbon nanotube structures. We see new processes that enable us to take the same technology we used to develop the transistor and apply it to making small-scale, precision mechanical devices that achieve new levels of performance because of the precision of the physical processing and achieve ultra-low cost associated with bulk processing techniques. The dimensions, geometry, and materials are all "engineered" to achieve truly optimal performance in all senses of the word.

The area I am thinking of specifically is called MEMS, or micro-electrical mechanical machines, pioneered by ARPA in the 1990s. (ARPA, or the Advance Research Project Agency, is the central research and development agency of the Department of Defense.) Early on, it was a technology in search of an idea or an application. Today, we are seeing MEMS finding their way into almost every product, from automobiles as airbag collision sensors, to cellular telephones as radio frequency filters, to Texas Instruments' light projector modulator chip, which is a silicone mirror device that tilts and projects images onto

163

screens with very high intensity, brightness, and resolution. We see this micro-mirror device being applied to building very precise mechanical resonating filters that are then miniaturized, finding their way into radio devices. We are beginning to see MEMS show up in advanced optical devices to provide optical switching for optical networks. So that technology, which is really an offshoot of our ability to process silicon with superb precision, has enabled a totally unrelated application and enabled a new market for optical switches. The combining of these precision silicone structures with microelectronic devices, such as sensors, transistors, and thermistors, into an integrated single chip, or "micro-system," will achieve significant gains in performance. In turn, this has allowed us to create new "micro-systems" to solve problems in different ways, better ways, more efficient ways, which leads to those new products and those new markets. I see this revolution continuing for the next 50 years.

People always say Moore's Law was a limit, a fundamental barrier to miniaturization, but every time we come close to it, we figure a new way to "cheat" Moore's Law (by shorter wavelength, phase masks, larger F number, etc.) and continue to move beyond it. Right now we are still a two-dimensional world. We are starting to reach the limit of where the device size can be measured now in the number of atoms. I believe we will now start to explore and develop that third dimension of integration. Today, that third dimension is fairly chunky. It is measured on the scale of hundreds of microns. We will improve those processes to the point where we will begin integration in that third dimension with more and more density, so that we will continue to push out the net of Moore's Law, and our electronics will continue to support the transistor revolution. I think this is precisely at the heart of a lot of our prosperity as a nation today, and we can trace much of our growth, productivity, and GDP back to microelectronics. In my opinion then, the transistor revolution still has a long way to go, probably another 20 years as we enter the age of "nanoelectronics."

Maintaining Competitive Advantages

There is no such thing as technology as a strategic weapon. I think technology advantage is about people, about ideas, and about adaptability to change. You can maintain a competitive edge as long as you are in the practice of creating new ideas. I go back to my professor's comment that physics is not a spectator sport. You have to be practiced. You have to be engaged in creating ideas, in developing intellectual property and applying that new intellectual property to today's problems and tomorrow's dreams. It is all continuously changing.

Think about an optical network switch today that is enjoying a dominant market share. A technology is just around the corner that is using a new generation of either lasers or MEMS. Optical switches will create a threat to that current system and allow another order of magnitude of improvement in performance, which will force the market to adopt the new technology. If you are not involved in that research, then you get left behind.

I think you see that happening in companies that operate in a fashion that does not enable them to create new technologies, so they end up acquiring other companies that have them. You have seen Cisco Systems do that by acquiring new ideas and new intellectual property, both by internal creation and by external acquisition. I think it's a matter of balance, of understanding the speed of technology devolution in the marketplace, the rate of technological evolution within your enterprise, the rate of technological evolution in competing enterprises, and the way you manage that change. Doing that well is what competitive advantage is really about.

Evaluating an Acquisition

If I were planning to acquire a company tomorrow, I would want to understand how the company values and manages technology. In doing so, I think it is important to look at and understand who their customers are and what their products are. How does technology play in their marketplace? How much do they depend on technology? How do they obtain that technology? Do they invent it? Do they acquire it? Do they barter for it? What is their strategy?

I would then look at the financials to see how efficient they are in managing that technology and bringing it to market. How efficient is that organization in managing its human resources, its people? How smart, how bright are their people in terms of technology? How happy are the people in their work environment? What is the longevity of the technology they have? How well is the intellectual property protected? How fragile is their technical solution in terms of stability within the marketplace? What new technologies, new ideas, and emerging disruptive technologies are they working on in the back room that might play? Are they aware of their competitors and their competitors' technology? Have they ever survived the emergence of a disruptive technology? I think the list of questions is very long. It is also a function of what kind of company you are trying to acquire. What is your motivation for that acquisition? Am I trying to fill a people gap? Am I trying to fulfill a disruptive technology threat, to mitigate that threat? Am I trying to buy market share? Am I trying to expand into new markets? Adjacent markets?

The important evaluation factors depend on what needs you are trying to fill, and what the strategy would be in terms of how the company would integrate with your enterprise. There are a lot of subjective factors in there too, for example, your workforce and how happy they are, how stable they feel. Some people don't like to work for a large corporation, so when you acquire a small company, you have to make sure that that intellectual enterprise is stable and not fleeting. You must seriously examine a great number of factors, and I have only begun to discuss a few of the thought processes that you would have to go through.

Risk

Good stewardship of an enterprise is based on good risk management. The key risk factors that I need to manage are schedule risk, cost risk, and technical viability risk. Among those three, you manage how to bring the new technology to market so that the investment costs are justified by the return on that investment due to the new technology. I can always operate faster by working in parallel, but that is going to cost more. I can try to develop it while minimizing annual costs by stretching it out, but I must be sure not to bring it to market so late that I lose the technical advantage. If the technology has a high technical hurdle, I may have to hedge the technology with multiple approaches to solve that same problem. If there are multiple solution space options –

that is, different ways to solve the problem, each with its own implications – I must be able to understand which is the right approach for my customer.

It is all about managing risk, managing schedule, managing cost, and working to achieve a near optimal balance among those competing choices. Your tools at hand to accomplish the task are ideas, money, time, and human capital. You can acquire technology by buying it from your competitor or by buying a small company. You can create the technology by investing in a university or your company. Or you can outsource the technology altogether and buy at the subsystem level.

In many of the systems we design, we build at the large-end user system level, so the systems are generally large and complex. You see that same trend now appearing in the electronics and communications industries. For example, Cisco Systems is a complex system designer and integrator, and the company builds very little in-house. For us, you only need to look at the international space station, the space shuttle, and all the communication satellites we have in orbit around the world. Look at the vast array of aircraft that we have built over the years. These are all examples of large, complex systems. There are innovation and intellectual property that have been developed over the years at every step of the way, and it is that intellectual property, that know-how, that defines you to your customers. You are constantly managing risk as you build these large, complex systems. Complexity is managed via design, redundancy, diversity of suppliers, and investments in new technology.

Best Technology Advice

As an experimentalist, I think back to my own experiences and am reminded of what Lewis Carroll wrote in his famous book, *Alice's Adventures in Wonderland:* "What I say thrice is truth." In technology terms, I would say you cannot assume anything in creating new things; instead, you must test, measure, and verify every behavior. I must test an object until I know it does what I think it does, and until I thoroughly understand the boundaries and the domains over which its behavior applies. I have always been a believer that a little skepticism is healthy, so I always like to verify and prove for myself what others have claimed. I will always believe the facts, but it is the theories that I have a hard time always accepting. That was at the core of my education as an experimental physicist. I believe science and engineering are not spectator sports. Doing things is the only way to be intellectually honest and to ground yourself in experience. I continually strive to improve my judgment, experience, and knowledge about science and technology, and I do so by being an active participant in the creative process.

Likewise, intellectual curiosity is important. You have to want to continuously learn. You have to want to innovate. You have to want to understand and explore new ideas and solutions. You don't do it in a vacuum; rather, you do it through a network of associates and team members within your company. We have more than 30,000 employees in our enterprise. A large portion of them are engineering and science-degree personnel. They have interests in everything from chemistry to engineering to physics to astrophysics. We try to stay connected and to be a community. We try to talk and to engage one another in ideas. In this job, we are continually getting exposed to new problems and ways to solve problems, whether it is a new class of aircraft, a new class of propulsion systems, new kinds of electronic devices, or communications devices. You are constantly choosing technical approaches to accomplish a specific project task; for example, in creating solutions for the "last mile" communications links, do you choose a laser communication link or a microwave communications link?

We need to gain understanding of the characteristics and issues for all these technologies to make the "near optimal" design. Experts in each respective field basically expose all these ideas to you. And the challenge is to gain an understanding while figuring out how the technology works in your application. I find the best way for me to absorb it is to ask questions while the experts are briefing me. If I push and prod enough, I can typically understand something fairly quickly. Once I understand how it works, I can usually apply it and know how to take advantage of it within our enterprise.

As technology applies in my day-to-day role as the CTO, it is important to remember that I set the vision and a course for our systems and the underlying technology. I am here to inspire others to reach for the stars and to help organize and focus the resources and energy of this enterprise on the right solutions and the best technology to solve the problems of our customers and our nation.

Fantasy Technologies

In my previous position as an office director at DARPA, I spent some time thinking about this issue: If I could create any new technology in the world, what would it be? I had the specific responsibility and charter to create new technologies and to prevent "technological surprise," so that our nation would not be caught at a disadvantage in confronting any adversary.

There are many boundaries in the physical world that, if broken, would truly change the world. This could be achieved by discovering a new physical phenomenon or a new physical understanding of the laws of physics that allows one to achieve a new effect or result. For example, I would like to find a way to break the speed of light, even if it is in an optically active material, or to find a new way to counter the force of gravity, even if only for a short time. Personally, I would like to create something new, something that really improves the world, an idea that would solve a fundamental problem we are facing or will face in the near future.

One idea I have been involved in is to create a new pure nitrogen chemical propellant, which holds the promise to yield two to three times more energy when reacted in a rocket engine. This would totally change the design of rockets and allow dramatically smaller rockets and larger payload into space. We are also working on a way to create a totally emission-free power generation technology that would avoid polluting the atmosphere. Both of these ideas would be disruptive technologies that, if possible, would change the entire world and the way things get done.

The Golden Rules

Technology is now an integral part of our world and promises to enable a world of discovery in the future. Look at the progress the human race has made over the last 100 years. We have gone from the discovery of an atom to understanding what an individual elementary particle is made of and the laws that govern them. We have developed the physics instruments enabling us to explore that whole domain of elementary matter. We have taken that understanding and developed instruments for the design and development of electronics and new materials. We have taken that understanding and generated the tools to allow us to build things, microelectronics.

We are now beginning to understand biology in the 21st century, in the same way that physicists came to understand the laws of nature in the 20th century. We will come to understand the human genome, and the complex proteins that define life itself. In the next hundred years, we will understand biology to the point where we will really be able to understand how a human is made. To me, that is the most remarkable thing.

In a matter of a thousand years, there are human minds that have come to be able to create the understanding and tools of mathematics, to discover the laws of physics, the fields of engineering, biology, and chemistry. We will come to truly understand life itself. I believe that is a remarkable achievement for human kind.

With that said, there really are no golden rules, except one: He who has the gold rules.

David Whelan joined Boeing as vice president and chief technology officer in 2001. Dr. Whelan is the top level executive within Space & Communications (S&C) of The Boeing Company, providing advice, counsel, and leadership to the president-S&C on technology matters covering all S&C programs and businesses. As the group's senior technology executive, he leads the group's "business of innovation" and ensures the functional excellence in the development of advanced, leading-edge technology for future aerospace transportation, surveillance, navigation, communications, and missile defense systems.

Before joining Boeing's Space & Communications, Dr. Whelan served as director of the Tactical Technology Office (TTO) of the Defense Advanced Research Projects Agency (DARPA) from 1996 to 2001. TTO *is chartered to research and develop leading-edge military technology across a broad range of aerospace, land, and weapon systems. As the director, Dr. Whelan was responsible for both the technical and financial aspects of TTO's $400 million annual budget. Before joining TTO, Dr. Whelan served from 1995 to 1996 as deputy director and then as acting director of DARPA's Sensor Technology Office, which develops advanced surveillance radars, fire control radars, and missile seeker technology for air defense systems.*

Dr. Whelan was honored in 2001 as the recipient of the Secretary of Defense Medal for Outstanding Civil Service and in 1998 as the recipient of the Secretary of Defense Medal for Outstanding Public Service for his innovation, design, and development of space-based surveillance and unmanned stealth combat aircraft. He has also received various other awards from Hughes Aircraft and Northrop-Grumman Corporations.

Dr. Whelan earned his Ph.D. in physics from the University of California at Los Angeles in 1983 and his Master of Science degree in Physics in 1978. He received his B.A. degree in 1977 from the University of California at San Diego.

TECHNOLOGY AS A STRATEGIC WEAPON

KEVIN VASCONI

Covisint

Chief Technology Officer

Success as a CTO

The most important thing a CTO needs to do is to drive business value or shareholder value by intelligently using technology to support whatever the business goals are. Our business is relatively straightforward; others are a bit more complex. In essence, not only do CTOs have to be the technology implementers and inventors, but we also have to be the technology advisors for the rest of the senior leadership team, in terms of the investments we make in technology to support corporate strategy. All of that revolves around the fact that we are an outstanding technology company, but we need to be a very profitable *and* an outstanding technology company.

One of the most important traits of a successful CTO has to be either a lust or passion for technology. That is tremendously important in technology leadership roles. You truly have to enjoy this business because it is tremendously demanding, and it takes a lot out of you and your family. If you don't like what you are doing, you are going to be miserable for the majority of your day because you *will* spend a majority of your day on your job. That's probably the first and foremost a trait. Another one is the desire to solve problems with technology and to use technology to advance the business.

How have I applied these traits over the course of my career? I think I've spent a lot of time at the office learning the business. The passion for technology has always led me to be more on the leading edge of technology, to be an early adopter of the technology, and to work with the business to figure out how we can use this technology to help advance the business and give it a competitive advantage.

Defining success as a CTO is not getting fired! There are a couple of dimensions to success. One of them is job satisfaction. Do you feel good about your contribution to the company? Do you feel good that both you and your technology organization are supporting the business over and above the cost the company incurs to keep you around? Those are definitely a measure of success. The other measures of success can be very specific, such as system up-time, systems availability, your security record in terms of attempted breaches, your application development cycle time, your organization's delivery record. On a very tangible basis, there are a few key metrics you can look at daily, weekly, or monthly that typically tell you if you are doing part of your job or not. The strategy part of your job isn't necessarily looking at a metric, but I think that metric correlates to the long-term success of your business (market share, profitability, growth, etc.).

Deciding on the Right Technologies

It is a challenge to decide between the cool technologies and the ones that are really necessary. Seven years ago, Web technology (not the IP part, but browser) was cool. Now it is part of your business. In fact, it is so ingrained in the business that many companies could not run without it. That vision was a very hard sell in most of corporate America in the early 1990s. The early adopters who got it right achieved a competitive advantage.

You want to stay abreast of the cool technologies and have a working knowledge of them. You want to let people in your organization who have a passion for those technologies experiment a little bit. You have to watch where the rest of the industry is going and then make your decisions. At the end of the day, cool technologies don't pay the bills, so I would personally err on the side of making sure it adds short-term value to the business. If it doesn't, then I wouldn't invest time or money in it unless I think there is some breakthrough opportunity.

To decide on the best technologies, you have to look at your current state of technology and where the business is trying to go. If your business is in a high-growth period, and rapid expansion of your computer systems is driving you, then you should look at technologies that are going to enable scalability while bringing time-to-market advantages. If your business is in a slow-growth phase or more static in nature, and you are having some operational issues, then you look at technologies that are more robust or proven. You may also have to challenge the underlying architecture of some of your products because you have to stabilize or scale the products.

The worst case is a functionally inferior product that requires "rearchitecting" to add the features or functions – that takes tremendous time to do right. And you will never get enough time, because your competition is not idle. You have to take your role as a businessperson, as well as a technologist, to try to figure out where the business is today and where it needs to go. The good news is that you have plenty of people in the business who have a good idea of where they want it to go – the CEO, the CFO, and the rest of the executive team.

Keeping Technologically Nimble

Being nimble technologically has a lot to do with the type of people you recruit and the culture of the organization you build. That is the only way I know how to do it. I know people who are great technical athletes, who can move with the technology as it morphs and migrates. To me, this passion to pursue technology is very important.

If you build an organization with thought leaders and strong people with those types of desires, you will, by definition, have a technologically nimble organization. The sub-culture there will drive you to stay current on the technology and drive you to use it in new and exciting ways. That's absolutely essential. Once you get the people, you have to create a culture that is going to thrive where people feel their creativity is valued, and they are allowed to make occasional mistakes. That keeps you nimble.

Future Pivotal Technologies

We are going to continue to see a substantial propagation of the Web-based technologies that we have to today. Next-generation IP will be very interesting; technologies that wring more and more bandwidth out of what we currently have will be a necessity as we move forward. Wireless technology has even greater potential. We will find some really breakthrough business applications for that. JAVA is here today and will be here tomorrow. It's a great tool. Web services – a combination of existing technologies in a slightly different delivery format – is probably the latest buzz on the horizon. It's going to be huge. There will be some interesting commercial and potentially legal issues around Web services, but I think there will be very high growth. That's what we will be reading about for the next five years – clever and nimble companies coming up with Web services.

Evaluating these new technologies takes two stages. First, you have to know whether that technology is pertinent and if it will help you solve a relative-term business problem. We do that via gap analysis and try to fill in the white space. Once you have identified a technology, then most companies have sophisticated methodologies for detailed analysis. This analysis should be very technically focused and very business focused – What are the real-world business parameters? It should also include a strategic look at the health of the supplier and any glimpse you can get into their vision of the future.

Integrating New Technologies

Integrating new technologies into your company begins with how good a job you did on the technology fit when you evaluated the technology company. It also has to do with both the culture of your company and that of the company you are going to work with. A lot of it goes back to whether the technology is needed by the business because that drives their need and desire for the technology. If you start with the fundamental premise of solving a business problem, you will see the technology pull through. That will make a lot of other issues go away. You can even make bad technology work if you have to solve a critical business problem.

The further you get away from how relevant the technology is to the business and your business partner, the harder the implementation becomes. Some of the problem centers around whether you can get the organization to understand what the technology will enable and why they need to make a change and invest in this technology solution. If you can successfully articulate that value proposition, you get a pull to a solution. Pulling technology through a system is a lot easier than pushing it through.

Top Issues

My top issues are in the top few of any CTO's issues list. It is my top two or three issues that I spend a majority of time working on – and a majority of my nights thinking about. Privacy and security in the Internet age are going to become more and more a part of all of our daily jobs. Businesses have to establish that trust with the customer and protect their privacy. They have to be diligent about the kinds of threats to all of us that exist in the electronic space that didn't exist five years before.

I worry about scalability and performance constantly. It is part of my company's value proposition. We have to deliver a satisfying customer experience. Ensuring customer satisfaction and security is so important. Another thing that worries me is capacity management and investment. How do I, as the guardian of the technology for my company, make sure that we invest that money to get the greatest return for the shareholders? It is one of my most critical functions. I have a huge budget and have to deliver that effectively and efficiently so we can add more customers at a very high customer satisfaction rate with the absolute minimum down-time. That takes investment. It's a balancing act.

Due Diligence and Risk Control

Conducting due diligence on a new company is as simple as rolling up your sleeves and talking to the people who are still there who built it on the technical side, and understanding how they designed and built the solution and what the level of investment has been. I would also look at how they perform on their systems availability and their security policy. You want to talk to the business owner and find out how he thinks the technology stack is supporting him. The last stop is to talk to some of the customers, especially your top few, and get their impressions of the product or technology that has been developed.

Controlling risk in technology is a managed process that analyzes risk and return. We pay attention to everything from significant statistical business analyses to a gut feel from 20 years in the industry. It's a tough thing to teach and learn. It also becomes part of the culture of an organization. You can see that in how it is manifested in a lot of companies. Do they make their release dates? Do they ship a quality product? It also comes down to what kind of project management skills you and your company have. At the end of the day, it's simple cost-benefit analysis including as many smart people in the analysis as possible.

Best Technology Advice

A couple of very wise people have mentored me. If you can find a great mentor, take full advantage of that relationship. Two other pieces of advice stick in my mind. One is that it is all right to make mistakes as long as you don't make them twice. That's a great piece of advice. If you can create a culture that is not so risk-averse and action-oriented, it's a very good thing. You can't build an organization that is punitive for people trying to do the right thing but who inadvertently make a mistake. We are human; we make mistakes. It's a reality of life. Individual and organizational character is measured by how you recover when you make that mistake. Shooting people doesn't help.

In his early EDS days, Ross Perot used to say, "If you see a snake, kill the snake." I think that is one of the best pieces of business advice I've ever heard. If people adopt that philosophy, and companies adopt that philosophy, they are bound to be highly successful. I think what he meant by it is that if you see a problem at your company, then you need to fix that problem because you, as a shareholder of that company, are responsible. It doesn't mean you have to fix everything yourself, but the concept that it is "somebody else's problem" is extremely detrimental to a company and to a culture.

The business advice that I espouse to other people on a personal level is to enjoy what you do. That is our number one recruiting question. My most common business advice is that if you are not using technology for a competitive advantage, you are at a disadvantage because somewhere, your competition is. It's a strategic weapon, and I have participated in some tremendous opportunities in terms of using technology as sustainable competitive advantage. You have to have enough knowledge of your business or industry to know where the pain points are and what your competition does well.

For me, the role of the CTO is to evaluate what technology is available that can widen the competitive advantage or create one. Then you need to look at what you have to do to sustain the competitive advantage, either by being early to market and not looking back, or by raising barriers to entry via investment or superior products.

Successful Team Building

What drives people to be CTOs is that they love technology. As you advance through the technology ranks, you find you could contribute more to the business if you could clone yourself. Unfortunately, that technology doesn't exist! The closest substitute I can see for that is to manage, develop, and nurture technical teams. The CTO is the ultimate embodiment of that, the person who loves technology and wants to solve more and more of those kinds of problems and to do so has to build teams. Teams turn into multiple teams, which turn into departments and then organizations. That is the thrill of it, the buzz – being able to oversee and guide a technology organization that is doing so many things that you as an individual couldn't possibly do alone.

Building those teams starts with recruitment. I recruit very good technology athletes and specialists. Especially in the senior management roles, you want good technology athletes. You want people who have proven track records in multiple technologies because that shows their ability to learn and implement a new technology, as well as their desire to learn new technologies when moving from job to job. As you move through the rest of the organization, you want specialists who are zealots in their particular technology. After that, you want a mix of experienced people and then fresh and eager youngsters that are excited and passionate.

Golden Rules

The number one golden rule of being a CTO is to never chase technology for technology's sake. Make sure you create an environment for your team that is constructively creative, and at the end of the day a fair and fun place to work. Do whatever you can to educate yourself and whatever allows you to understand the business to the best of your ability. Simply have fun! Enjoy what you are doing.

Given the right people and time, anything can work. Ensure the technology supports the business, and pull technology through – don't push it.

The Future of Technology

Technology in the next five years will change at least as radically as we have seen in the last five years. I think there will be one or two breakthrough technologies that will touch society the same way the Internet has touched us all.

The rate of change is not going to speed up, but I don't think it is going to slow down. There are no indications that innovation is waning. Some of the technologies we have now didn't even exist five years ago. Over the next five years, we will be working with technology that was only a gleam in someone's eye today – hopefully mine.

Kevin Vasconi is the chief technology officer and senior vice president, Technology, for Covisint. He is responsible for overseeing construction of the exchange and its technology development.

Before joining Covisint, Mr. Vasconi was part of the senior management team that formed Auto-Xchange, an Internet B2B joint venture between Ford and Oracle, where he served as chief technology officer. Prior to that, he spent more than ten years at Ford holding several technical management positions, including chief technology officer for Ford's Consumer Connect Group.

Previously, Mr. Vasconi held several technical and engineering positions at Allen-Bradley and General Motors. He holds a Bachelor of Science degree in technology from Purdue University.

THE ROLE OF THE CTO IN A VENTURE-BACKED STARTUP

DAN BURGIN

Finali

Chief Technology Officer

The Role of the CTO

There are potentially many different roles a CTO can play in a company. Indeed, the title CTO itself is a rather recent phenomenon in business, and the position still takes many different forms, usually depending on the size and type of company. Startups have very different needs from established companies, depending on their market focus, funding life cycle, and whether or not the technology the company uses is part of their intellectual property or not. For instance, my company has proprietary technology that we use to differentiate ourselves from our competitors and that, as opposed to managing licensed software only, has a big impact on the demands and focus of the job. For example, I spend a good deal of time working with patent attorneys and other lawyers, filing and protecting our various patents. Obviously, if we licensed all our software, as opposed to writing and creating it, I would not need to do that.

Additionally, since this is a venture-backed startup, the CTO role here is quite strategic and market-focused, and I spend much of my time trying to position our technology and leading a very forward-thinking group of architects, engineers, and designers doing research and development-oriented activities. CTOs in organizations without intellectual property software as a key component of their company tend to focus on larger business issues and on the details of technical operational issues, rather than looking at the companies' strategic possibilities and intellectual property protection issues.

There are unique issues for a CTO in a startup backed by venture capital and not yet profitable. The CEO and president of my company rely on me as CTO to position and deliver the companies' software and technical services, so we can reach profitability as soon as possible and reduce the need and frequency of additional funding rounds. This is particularly vital to the success of a company – and especially so in tight economic times. Let me give an example of exactly how this manifests itself.

Software development in a startup is always a game of trade-offs. Good development philosophy, or at least traditional philosophy, dictates comprehensive processes. These processes tend to slow development cycles, especially for organizations like ours, with the constant problem of too few developers. The pressure to minimize cash burn dictates that we must trade off things that can increase the risks to our product. For instance, comprehensive functional requirements, design specifications, design reviews, and even code reviews become bullet-pointed presentations at a few meetings as the means to convey the design goals and structures to the team, rather than the traditional deliverables in the form of detailed documents. While this is risky, it allows speed-to-market, a critical factor for driving revenue quickly and lowering cash burn.

Incidentally, I've read many of the books on development philosophy that preach that lost time due to poor process is higher than lost time due to implementing good, documented process. But practical experience is a ruthless teacher; it has shown me the payoff is high for taking these risks, and they can be successfully navigated. I say navigated rather than managed because while it's not easy, it can be done, only with a great team. There is no management substitute for communicative and talented engineers and managers who can succeed – even thrive – in the chaos of a startup.

Another example of risk navigation unique to software companies who host and manage software on behalf of clients is scalability. This issue presents several interesting trade-off possibilities and can be particularly difficult to juggle.

Managed software solutions, hosted by the vendor – as is the case with our company – tend to come to market with issues around scalability. The early-stage releases of software can often have bottlenecks that take time to work out and cause issues with scalability. While the solution must deliver for the client and adhere to service level agreements for uptime and speed, there are trade-offs that can be made. Usually this means throwing additional hardware at the problem early on. The down side is the operating costs associated with running the software. More development time focused solely on scalability can decrease the cost of operating the software by lowering hardware needs, but it also tends to slow the all-important feature releases, which extend the product's attractiveness to clients.

The issue is managing risks: Too little focus on scalability, and the operating costs are too high. Too much focus on scalability, and the product attracts fewer buyers. I usually focus the team on sales and balance the richness of the sales pipeline against the operating costs. If we can achieve a kind of stasis where the finance folks are not clamoring for hardware cost reductions, and sales are still flowing, we have successfully balanced and navigated these issues.

Using Technology for Business

Technology is a business tool, and as a businessperson, I believe CTOs should strive not to solve technology problems, but to solve business problems by using technology. A startup CTO must focus as an executive in the company on the business problems of the company and how technology can effectively and efficiently solve these problems.

Too often, especially in larger corporations, technology departments have developed philosophies that appear to me as simply empire-building. A lot of these departments have what is commonly termed a "not invented here" mindset, meaning they feel they have to own or build every piece of technology their company uses, and they will license only the software that fits and extends this empire-builder mindset. I think that's a mistake – and ultimately it harms the competitive position of the company. There's a serious lack of business-success focus, and instead a focus on building a technology empire. There are so few internal software initiatives that succeed – it's really shocking. Companies, even relatively young companies, become mired in legacy from this empire-building and, as a result, seem frozen in time, technically. Even simple initiatives that could pay tremendous competitive dividends cannot be successfully implemented because they must fit the goals of the empire, not the goals of the company.

Too few executives feel comfortable challenging the IT group to deliver, fearing doing so will endanger existing revenues, and the cycle perpetuates itself. CTOs are in a unique position to constantly challenge the empire-builders, and non-technical executives must likewise challenge the CTO to deliver on this role for the company.

Technological Innovation Slowdown

Technical innovation really suffered once the Internet bubble burst. It's a different pace now and one that, if allowed to slow too much, could harm the entire world economy.

Think about the tremendous value the technology investment boom of the last decade has had on driving the U.S. economy – even the world economy. America went from massive debt to budget surplus in the span of a few short years, largely on the back of technology investment – especially Internet investment. The level of innovation, sadly, will be challenged as investors shy away from funding good teams with good ideas. Small companies are built and succeed on the applicability of their innovation, and often in large companies, this level of innovation is smaller because the company is simply too large – not to mention too much of a technical empire – to innovate effectively.

Innovation requires passion and risk navigation, and that will get you fired in many large companies. Smaller organizations tend to reinvent business strategies and the application of technology as a way to outperform their larger, industry-leading competitors. This innovation and risk-taking push larger companies to license these applications, or innovate more aggressively internally. This cycle of competitive innovation is the fuel of our economy, and it's one of the things that make capitalist economies so strong. Struggling countries need innovation and entrepreneurialism more than anything else – even money. And America needs innovation to keep our economy, and indeed the world economy, growing.

While there has definitely been a slowdown, there is still innovation going on, although it's different. A lot of the technologies I see being employed right now are tried-and-true. The level of risk-taking in corporations has gone down, and investors are tight with investment dollars for startups. During these down periods, companies are looking to weather the storm, and larger companies with existing revenue streams are going to improve more slowly and be more risk-averse, and therefore innovate even less. These business cycles eventually turn, and investment dollars start to flow again – there is simply too much money to be made from innovation for it to ever stop – thank goodness.

Choosing the Right Technologies

Companies really don't need cool technologies. What they need are business solutions, and technology is usually only a part of that. An example from my industry is customer relationship management and customer care. Customer care is often seen as a cost center, a necessary expense to operate the business, but it can be a revenue center if done well and done differently. The problem is that CRM (customer relationship management) also includes customer-focused business philosophy, and a lot of the technology departments that implement customer relationship initiatives are failing because they focus solely on the technology, and don't embrace the non-technical philosophies of the solution.

There are industry reports that more than 50 percent of internal CRM initiatives, in both large and small organizations, are failing. One big reason is that the decisions being made are about cool technology and empire-building, not about the full range of technical and non-technical issues that are required to succeed. Unfortunately, many technology departments in organizations are only as relevant as the technology they deploy, and that's really a shame. That is the fault of CTOs and CIOs, neglecting to correctly position their solutions with operational groups in the company.

CRM is about technology, but it's also about embracing the business practices of lowering costs and raising revenues, and of changing the way you do business – not just implementing cool technologies. This is a pervasive problem in technology departments across corporate America. It represents a competitive opportunity for startups to exploit.

The Mindset of a CTO

Technology people use a couple of traditional measures for success. One is return on investment, or ROI. That is sufficient for some kinds of technologies, but there are a lot of technology decisions where you can see an ROI relatively fast – but still fail to solve the business problem. You can recoup the cost of a software application relatively fast, within a quarter or two, but the benefit to the corporation is in advancing the companies' ability to create revenue, to create value for shareholders. Simply recouping the value of a software application is rarely enough.

I tend to have my team focus on the speed of "time to benefit," rather than on just ROI in evaluating solutions. And it isn't just about dollars; it's about creating a different mindset for the business using the technology. Paying for the software is a good measure, but it's only one measure. I try to look at how we can reap new revenue with the solution, or reap a cost-savings of a solution by increasing efficiency, for instance. Many software solutions have paid for themselves, only to leave other opportunities lying on the floor. Again, I often observe this when technologists focus on the technology only and not the wider business solution.

I also think an important mindset for a CTO is to nurture the creativity of the technology teams. Generally, this means creating as non-political a workplace as possible. New ideas come from all corners of a business, and I try to keep my door open as much as possible to encourage discussion. I try to listen to and probe on ideas that come to me, and if I latch onto something, it's critical that I allow the benefit of this idea to be credited to the person who came up with it. Executive teams and boards tend to focus only on the top tiers of the company, and too often the people who actually create these ideas do not get credit. Not only is this wrong, but it eventually will harm a companies' ability to compete and to attract top talent. Companies are only as good as their people, and taking this merit-based mindset as a CTO pays huge dividends, both for the company and for the shareholders. It's a key lever a CTO can pull to create a great company.

Keeping a Company on the Cutting Edge

Many corporations implement proprietary technology. Open architectures, and even more importantly, standards-based technology, are very vital in staying nimble. For example, you could create a technology empire like Microsoft by creating new standards, but you cause incredible amounts of waste in the rest of the industry. It's a very bad corporate citizen kind of policy. It's also a very difficult path to take. Very few companies can be that proprietary and succeed.

The vast majority of companies have to embrace standards-based technology and open architecture. Not to pick on Microsoft, but they have created a completely dominant product in Internet Explorer. It is the customer interface to the Web in a lot of ways. There are open technologies, standards-based technologies, that Microsoft ignores. I think eventually that practice will be to their own detriment. As a business person, I do understand the competitive impulse to create the standard, the thinking being, "Create the standard and you lead; adopt an existing standard and you follow." But if you can build technologies that allow you to leverage standards-based technology and implement those technologies, as well as to uphold those standards, I think it's better for the health of the entire industry. Altruistic, I know.

But just think about the billions and billions of dollars that have been spent trying to make Web-based applications compatible with the two dominant browsers – Internet Explorer and Netscape – neither of which adheres to the standards as they've been written by standards bodies such as the World Wide Web Consortium (W3C). That's a huge waste and ultimately hurts everyone. It's a huge weight on companies that have to create Web applications, as they must try to make their applications work with these browsers that absolutely defy all standards and work completely differently. It is arguably a good competitive strategy for these companies, but it is truly wasteful for everyone else and lowers the level of innovation and the advance of technical solutions. While it is an unfortunate and harmful side effect of modern business, I believe it is here to stay.

Dominant Technologies

Java has a really strong foothold, and there are terrific benefits to using technologies like Java to compete. Companies that standardize around reusable architectures and formats give themselves very useful flexibility. All companies migrate their business model over time, and software code that is flexible enough to operate in many different environments and extensible against many different types of business goals is invaluable. You don't want to spend two years and $20 million developing software that can't run on a different platform – that's just stupid, as these platforms migrate around in terms of strengths and weaknesses. There are limitations to development environments like

Java, but I think Java and its cousins in other forms are the things that companies ought to embrace and standardize around.

There are also data exchange formats that are becoming extremely important in keeping a company's configuration data and data-passing capabilities open and flexible. XML (eXtensible Markup Language) has become incredibly important. A key strategy for my company has been the use of XML as a data-passing architecture. We've moved this data transmission architecture away from the application architecture to great advantage. Our application, like many, requires client-by-client customization, and by moving these customizations out of the application code and into XML, we've dramatically shortened implementation cycles, reduced the pressure on version releases, and simplified maintenance. This should be a standard practice of Internet-based architectures, as it also allows easy integration and data-passing between disparate applications without the need for heavy API-level integration or the incredibly powerful but cumbersome integration technologies like COM or CORBA.

By embracing XML and Java very aggressively, our company has reaped big dividends for us as inexpensive commodity hardware architectures evolved to run our Web services in inexpensive server clusters. That we'd written our core applications in Java and separated our data-passing and customization architectures into XML allowed us to very quickly reach time-to-benefit with our product and get to market effectively.

Important Concerns for the Future

There's been a lot of hype around wireless and not a lot of reality-based thinking about wireless initiatives. Other countries have certainly proved wireless can be a viable business environment. Japan, for instance, has more wireless phones than wired phones.

By creating the telephone infrastructure in this country, we have a legacy that, in a way, we don't want to give up. Countries that would have been seen as behind in terms of building that wired infrastructure, have now leapfrogged us with innovations of their solutions within the wireless space.

Things are coming along that I see as very important. For example, the Bluetooth standard allows wireless communication between two devices – say, a headset that is the entire wireless phone interface. The hardware of your phone would be perhaps woven into your belt. You just wear your phone with you, but you never access the phone, except through the Bluetooth standard headset device; you carry in your pocket the wireless device that is basically just a headset. You can hook it on your ear and dial the number, and you have a wireless phone with you at all times that is very small and very flexible.

I think there are all sorts of solutions around another standard there, the Bluetooth standard, and it is really important because it allows all companies to create products that will be brought to the marketplace by a broad range of vendor technologies. Again, there is a standards-based movement that creates tremendous business innovation opportunities because of the standard itself and the interoperability the standard enables.

Implementing Technologies

The important thing about technology is the people who use it. It has to be accessible; it has to be consumable relatively quickly; and you can't have a long learning curve on a technology and expect it to be widely embraced by either the people in your organization or your customers.

Technologies have human interfaces that are critical to their success. Whenever we implement a new technology, I pay particular attention to the end user. As a contact center company, we have customer care agents who use this technology to interact with our clients. If they don't understand how the technology works – if it's slow, if it's a confusing interface, if it's hard to use – all these things factor into the adoption rate. Technology without a high adoption rate is doomed. I try to spend a lot of time listening to end-users, with an eye to making sure they understand the technology and that it actually works for them – that it solves the business problem we set out to solve, and that we did not just create a cool technology that nobody will use.

There is a tangential issue here. I believe human-machine interfaces are the next big opportunity on the Web. The Web is so new, and it's such a new paradigm that we have applied a lot of our old ways of thinking to the Web. Primarily the view has been to take somewhat mature interfaces, such as PC interfaces, and expand them to the Web. What works on the Web is really conversation, and a PC interface has almost none of that. The technologies that have been most embraced on the Web have been things like e-mail and chat rooms, things that are ongoing, human-to-human interactions through the media of the Internet. Things that don't work on the Web are things that are antithetical to conversation, like filling out forms on Web sites. It is the opposite of a conversational interface. It's a cold, hard, boring, often confusing task – a highly non-human interface. Forms interfaces can be very user-unfriendly. Human-machine interfaces have been talked about in the social sciences a lot and are a particular passion of mine.

Every Web site has a user interface, a design, a hierarchy, and a learning curve. As a user, if you want to do business with that Web site, you have to climb that learning curve and understand that interface. You have to understand the mental model of how that Web site is constructed and how to get the most out of it with the least amount of effort. Conversational interfaces are a way to standardize a Web site and lower the barriers of learning to climb that interface. No instructions required, one problem at a time – as if your best technical buddy were sitting with you all the time as you traverse the site.

Human-machine interfaces, conversational and socially intelligent interfaces, are a huge opportunity for designers of applications and Web sites. It's the kind of thing that people haven't focused on very much. Retail Web sites are wondering why they have 95 percent abandonment of shopping carts on their site. Just compare a brick-and-mortar store to the Web site. You get to the point in the real store where you want to ask the salesperson a question. But on the Web site, there's nobody to ask. Human-machine interfaces are so poor right now, and there is so much that could be done that isn't being done to change the entire paradigm of human-machine interaction. It's an incredibly exciting opportunity for the technology industry.

Best Advice

I try to gather as much critical feedback from the technology groups I manage as I can. One of these efforts once uncovered a great bit of advice about leadership. As technologists, we talk about scaling applications and servers all the time, but we rarely consider that the same dynamics apply to human beings. CTOs want to have their hands on as many things as they can. But it doesn't work – you don't scale.

You have to delegate; you have to allow the people who run your organization to have three things: authority, responsibility, and accountability – in that order. It's not enough to give someone responsibility and hold them accountable – you have to also give them the authority to succeed. If you're a director or manager in a company, you have to have the authority to make hard decisions, to make tough calls, to actually move the process forward without the input of a hundred people or, worse, the entire executive team. The best advice I've ever received from managing technology is to try to stay out of the way at critical moments. This builds confidence in the manager and in the team and allows for much better scaling of the organization.

I would give two pieces of advice. One is to embrace standards. If there's a choice of writing something yourself or embracing a standard as a shortcut, always choose to embrace the standard. It will pay dividends later on. It always does. You can't create a new standard, especially as a non-dominant company. If you're Microsoft, maybe you can get away with it, but in 99 percent of companies, if you don't embrace the standard when you have the opportunity, you're going to end up having to rewrite it later on.

The second piece of advice is to constantly challenge your own "not invented here" perspective. It's so easy to think you can build everything yourself. Often, it's not the right choice. But, if there's a licensable technology or even a freeware application you can integrate into your environment to speed things up, you should – especially as a startup CTO. Speed is so important, especially in the short business cycle, that constant evolution of technology that we have now. Speed is your enemy. Time is money, and money is the thing you have the least of. So embrace standards, and if you can license it, then license it.

Golden Rules of Being the CTO

Don't take yourself too seriously. You're in a position of a lot of power and influence. Use that influence to empower other people. I feel a lot of technology decisions get made at the top management levels of companies, and that is usually the worst place to make important technical decisions. Companies are often dictatorships, when they really should be meritocracies, where the best idea wins. The reason for that is that you create an army of entrepreneurs – innovators who believe if they come up with a great idea, they don't have to fear that presenting that idea will either get it stolen from them or will get them ridiculed. In a meritocracy, the best idea should always win. It's a hard ideal to live up to because so often companies can't move forward without some dictatorship-like decisions, but it's a noble goal, and it pays such dividends if you can pull it off.

The Future of Technology

I don't think we're done with the innovation on the Internet. The Internet is barely functioning as a technical innovation platform. It has had a tremendous boost because it was a completely new channel for doing business. Investment cycles, stock bubbles, and IPO frenzies aside, we aren't even close to finished here. The amount of innovation that can be done using the Internet is the Industrial Revolution of our time. It isn't over. We're simply being caught up in a normal economic downturn that is an unfortunate side effect of human nature, nothing else, and that will turn around, we hope very quickly, encouraging investment dollars to flow back into small, innovative startup companies.

I think technology will continue to transform the way businesses function and enterprises compete. We're just at the beginning of the e-business revolution. It has just started, no matter what's happening in the investment markets. There's a lot more to come.

Recently named to InfoWorld's Advisory Council and Top 100 CTO Network, Finali vice president, CTO, and co-founder Dan Burgin has been professionally involved with the Internet since its advent.

Before co-founding Finali Corporation, Mr. Burgin managed product development for Infonautics Corporation, where he designed implementation architectures for international expansion and led the conception, design, and development of Infonautics' Internet products. Earlier, Mr. Burgin was director of Technology at KnowledgeFlow, an enterprise application service provider that targeted online banking. There, Mr. Burgin led interactive-media project development for such Fortune 1000 Corporations as American Express and CoreStates Bank.

LEADING TECHNOLOGY DURING TURBULENT TIMES

FRANK CAMPAGNONI

GE Global eXchange Services

Chief Technology Officer

Characteristics of a Successful CTO

As the top executive in a company, the chief technology officer serves as the focal point for where the business and technology strategies converge. The CTO acts as that intersection point in a company where the business models, objectives, and strategies coalesce with the technology strategies and infrastructure required to make that business successful.

Many qualities are essential to being a successful CTO – particularly during these turbulent technology times – such as in-depth technical knowledge and confidence. You must be a very strong businessperson, as well. If you're going to assume a technical role within an organization, you need to be able to match the technology strategy to the business objectives. The CTO should be very balanced, in terms of strengths, on the business side and the technology side.

Another important but intangible key to a top CTO entails serving as a visionary. Clearly, the ability to set the right vision represents a critical element to being a solid CTO, and it has become a prerequisite for the job. Vision enables the CTO to formulate an abstract model of the future of a technology architecture or platform. At least for me, specifically, it really requires visualization. Such a conceptual model allows you to see, feel, and touch. This ability to manipulate in your mind a model of the future in terms of an ultimate objective – or at least from an abstract sense, the qualities necessary to achieve the ultimate objective – is vital. Ultimately, technology is a journey, not a destination. No magic end-point exists. It will continuously change and evolve; nonetheless, certain underlying principles guide the organization and its technical capabilities. The visualization ability greatly enhances the aim to manipulate models internally, so they are both robust and forward-thinking.

A CTO also needs to be fairly charismatic, because a large part of the technology role requires cross-functional activity, regardless of whether the engineering department works for the CTO. The CTO will never have all the staff needed, and it will always be a very small proportion of people. As a result, the CTO needs to exhibit a very strong personality, be charismatic, and communicate well because a lot of what you do demands evangelism. You affect change by creating and communicating a vision, so employees become motivated to achieve that vision. Many personal traits go along with the chief technology position due to the cross-organizational nature of the occupation. If you lack the ability to communicate and evangelize, it makes the job much more difficult.

The Role of a Successful CTO

Success as a CTO heavily depends upon the success of the business. Many of the same metrics used to measure the success of the business are metrics we use to measure our success. As the technology organization, our mission centers on achieving the broader business objective; if the business metrics and objectives are not met, then we're not achieving our goals, either. Underneath that, we look for areas in which we can provide very substantive uptake of the various initiatives within the business.

An example within GE Global eXchange Services (GXS) revolves around the use of the Internet for business-to-business electronic commerce. As we see the portion of the revenue that the business generates increasing in that area, we are able to meet a core business objective. We look for the opportunity to provide very explicit impact on the business objectives and metrics through the different technology initiatives. Clearly, the Internet is one of them. Our supply-chain collaboration application works over the Internet, as well as the data interchange. We can measure the revenue, the uptake, and the reliance of the business on the technology initiatives, which in turn serve as measures of our success. Ultimately, we're successful if the business is successful, so we use many of the same metrics you would use for any business to indicate our success: the revenues, the profitability of the business, and the growth of the business.

In our marketplace, we must constantly stay attuned to evolutions and changes in technology, since rapid changes in technology can have an impact on our business. I spend a lot of time researching and reading the literature, watching the trade press, talking to other people in the industry, and going to conferences to constantly gauge technology developments. I must stay up-to-date with current and planned

199

advances and identify their impacts on our business, which certainly represents a critical focus for me.

It is a very challenging task to keep a company technologically nimble, particularly given so much innovation and upheaval within our industry. Yet I believe that must be part of my role – to always be on the leading edge.

Part of my job requires driving new technologies back into the organization, to work with the senior leadership within GE Global eXchange Services and inform them about key technical trends within the industry. In turn, our leadership evaluates technologies' impact on our business and why they are important for us. I outline how these technologies provide new channels and new ways for us to make our services available and potentially increase our revenue and profitability. Part of my job is to encourage that kind of thinking by the staff, which explains why we have a distinction between the CTO and the vice president of Engineering.

The engineering VP position is a very execution-oriented role – developing products and services – while my job looks out on the horizon to think about new strategies and work with my team to experiment. Then I drive that back into the organization through the leadership team and technical vitality opportunities for the engineering group. We collaborate on these new technologies and identify ways they apply to our services. Finally, my group remains very involved in driving the incorporation of these technologies into our products and services. So we serve as a consulting organization in many ways to help other organizations within our business figure out how we actually incorporate support for these capabilities into our products and services.

Another key element to any technology organization is the talent in that area – both attracting and retaining very experienced and technically competent people to work in the engineering and the CTO's organizations. We must grow the technical vitality of the teams and provide the kinds of experiences and discourse that keep people on the top of their game, ensure they are constantly honing their skills, and challenge them to learn new technologies to stay ahead of the curve.

A third important area entails monitoring the marketplace to understand how our technical aims correlate to the activity in the business-to-business electronic commerce marketplace, which also evolves and shifts regularly. Such perspective allows us to evolve our technical infrastructure and business model to provide the greatest value for our customers. The market is very important, and I spend a lot of time understanding how the technologies and the infrastructure we develop can be applied in new and innovative ways to solve customer business problems.

Choosing the Right Technology

One of the golden rules of technology states that everything must serve a business purpose. Technology because it is "neat" does not imply relevance to a business. Many really cool technologies out there have the potential to deliver significant business impact. In a business-to-business context, it is critical to understand how the business process melds with the technology. It is a bad idea to automate a process just for the sake of automating it. You have to look at how the technology can profoundly change or benefit a process. Because of the important feedback loop between technology and business, you may need to reengineer a process before you automate it.

Some of the changes we continue to see with the Internet highlight this issue very strongly. Certainly, the Internet represents a very interactive technology. Many capabilities of the Internet were specifically designed to provide interactive and real-time data transfer, interactions, collaborations, and negotiations. That is different from the computing model that existed 25 years ago, which still exists in many businesses' information technology systems through a batch-oriented model. Businesses have traditionally exchanged information by a store-and-forward model. Now a whole new set of technologies has emerged. Instead of taking our business processes as they exist, many of which were built around store-and-forward processing, we need to reengineer processes to take advantage of advances in technology.

As a service-focused business, GXS doesn't generate a lot of our revenue selling software, and the software we do sell is intended to help integrate business with our services infrastructure. On top of having a service-based model, we are a service provider to trading communities. This means any business, in bringing a product or service to market, interacts with lots of other businesses: their suppliers, marketing and sales executives, and, of course, all the hands that touch the product or think through the service as it winds its way to the market – in other words, the entire supply chain. Our role is to provide capabilities that facilitate the electronic interactions between these business partners, whether those interactions are exchanging crucial business information, procuring materials they need (either to manufacture their products or keep their businesses running), collaborating on design, or coordinating promotions management.

In addition to providing supply-chain capabilities, we provide an enormous amount of value for these communities as an aggregator of information. We can put two trading partners together and help them interact, but we can use that same infrastructure to help connect any trading partner with any other trading partner. Such a many-to-many architecture allows us to act as a switching mechanism to interconnect any company with any other company. In addition to providing value, we think we derive an enormous amount of value and power from this model, as well. The combination of elements – namely the aggregation of relationships within a community, the content within the community, and the ability to easily interconnect any member of that community with any other member, even though they might not have joined our network to trade with one another, is very powerful. Envision the business model as a vortex around which trading communities are assembled and combined, with GXS providing services that facilitate their interactions. Our infrastructure supports the very secure, reliable, and high-performance interactions among those businesses.

Within this model, certain technologies become important, while others do not. Our business has shifted its focus to being almost exclusively based on the Internet because we know that is where the e-commerce industry is going. So the technologies we offer need to be Internet-related, well-suited for a service-based model and supportive of a many-to-many model. Based on these criteria, we can focus on areas of technology that are most applicable to our commerce platform. Within that sphere, we have our own architectural model based on standards, such as Java, directory services, and security standards, that are quite pervasive on the Internet – but they are assembled in a particular way to support a many-to-many model of interactions between trading partners. Our due diligence checklist allows us to evaluate applications or technologies that we might want to bring into our environment and see how well they integrate with our security model, our community management model, and our application integration model. The checklist helps us put a filter on the universe of technologies and select the ones most applicable to our business model.

I have been involved in several acquisitions and participated in the due diligence process that accompanied each purchase. One of the primary criteria for our business in any acquisition is that we have a very specific model of how our commerce platform works and the way things integrate with that platform. So from a technical due diligence side, we pay particular attention to certain aspects of the technology we would acquire.

Community management represents a very critical area for our business. As a service provider, our foundation supports the many-to-many model, which allows interactions within business communities and facilitates the sharing of members between business communities. We must allow for the fact that these communities evolve and shift, which means they both gain and lose members over time. It is not a static situation, but very dynamic, and it needs to be carefully managed to ensure protection of intellectual property and information. There needs to be an underlying infrastructure that provides very strong capabilities to manage accessed information, to ensure that people see the information who have permission to see it, and to make certain that others cannot see information that they are not permitted to access. There also needs to be a dynamic ability to provision and manage the trading community. In one form or another, every technology has some form of community management. How do you put a user in your system? How do you manage the security? How do you manage the roles and rights of that user?

Security is a second key area of focus. How do you manage security? What is the model for security? How can security be maintained over the Internet? How does the data remain secure? How do you authorize an individual or company to have access or not have access to certain data? Typically, you find a hierarchical model of roles, responsibilities, and access, and then a set of technologies that go around that model to ensure the system is secure and that there is an authorization and authentication of the users. The system must maintain this separation of authority to access certain information and not access other information.

The integration layer represents a third important area. Just about every technology will have ways of integrating with other systems, using external interfaces that allow information to be imported or exported from that system. We are very interested in the kinds of capabilities those external interfaces provide, their data formats, and the best manner possible to integrate other applications and exchange information within that technology.

System management is the final core focus for us. We maintain a very large commerce platform with billions of transactions running through it; we must be able to efficiently and effectively manage the platform to understand the health of the application and the technology.

The Impact of the Internet

The Internet continues to have a profound impact on all kinds of interactions; for example, business-to-consumer and business-to-business will evolve and incorporate new technologies and capabilities as time passes. Five to ten years from now, I see business-to-business interactions as very similar to what we see in the financial markets now, where you have program trading and huge efficiencies in the markets. In the future, these technologies and standards are going to evolve to the point where there will be seamless interconnectivity between businesses, and enormous transparency in terms of the information on which businesses operate. This development will have a large impact on the efficiencies and effectiveness of our markets and business-to-business commerce. I think we will see program trading systems heavily influence business-to-business. Business will be largely automated, run by a lot of machine-to-machine interactions. Humans will always be a part of the equation, but I think there will be huge volumes of automated interactions, which will have tremendous impact on the liquidities and efficiencies of our markets.

Web services represent an emerging and high-focus area in our business. This is a set of technologies evolving on the Internet where service providers can make their capabilities available through industry standard interfaces. Other companies can leverage these capabilities and combine them in ways to provide services to end-users. A company might not provide any of those customer-facing services themselves, but they can use those services in unique and innovative ways to provide value to their customers. We are very focused on learning as much as we can about Web services technologies and in prototyping and providing ways that our services can be used through those interfaces.

Web services technology is vital to us as a service provider because it provides a conduit, a way of exposing our capabilities so they can be readily used and consumed by people. This development will be critical to the future of our business. It provides a new channel and a vehicle to our service delivery. One of the issues we have struggled with as we move to the Internet is that being the end provider of everything takes an enormous amount of resources. A lot of our capabilities are focused around the aggregation of the community, the content, the management, and the commerce platform that we have – which is very high-availability, high-transactive-volume, and very secure – not necessarily focusing on the end-user experience as much. It takes a lot of resources to be able to provide all the capabilities. Our customers always want more than we can possibly deliver. Through the Web services model, we can make our core competencies available and allow other people to provide the plethora of applications that supply-chain partners can use to interact with each other. Web services can innovate in previously unimagined ways.

One of the technologies involved in Web services is eXtensible Markup Language (XML), on which, of course, we were very focused before a lot of the Web services technologies began to evolve. One of the focuses we have on XML is related to our role as a data-interchange service provider. In that role, a core part of our business allows us to help businesses to exchange crucial business information with each other. XML serves as a very important technology for exchanging information because it is a way of formatting information that can be read by both humans and computers. It is a very powerful mechanism for data exchange. XML allows a lot of intelligence to be put inside of

205

the information, as well as used in the processing of that information – whether done by a human using a Web browser or via a computer-to-computer interaction. I think XML will continue to be a very important technology for us because it adds a whole new level of capability and power in terms of the exchange and processing of information.

XML will also be very important to the industry because so much information will be unleashed through XML formats. In fact, I believe that the proliferation of XML will lead to a resurgence in the notion of intelligent agents. This is kind of a science-fiction term for computers that can do smart processing. I think what we will see over time is an emergence of these smart programs that are able to go out – now that information is available in a way that computers can sort through – and find things that are relevant and even act on that information. I think the use of XML to encode all the available information on the Internet will lead to new, more powerful intelligent agents, which are probably going to be used in the business-to-consumer space, but clearly are going to be more important in business-to-business. As businesses want to automate more of their interactions over the Internet, these powerful computer programs will start to emerge and will process a lot of the information that is now available in XML.

Using Technology Strategically

An essential tool of the CTO involves the abstract model of the information technology system. We have built a commerce platform in the course of the last three-and-a-half years that I have been at GE, and it is assembled entirely out of off-the-shelf, open systems technology, such as Java, lightweight directory access protocol, and X509 (a security standard). The platform components are all widely available, standards-based technologies. We have taken great pains not to incorporate a lot of proprietary technology into our infrastructures. The key for us is the way the platform has been assembled using a many-to-many model and a service-based architecture, plus implementation by provisioning.

An example from telecom can be helpful in illustrating the concept of provisioning. When you as a customer order new services from the telephone company (such as three-way calling, voice mail, and call waiting), the telephone company doesn't build you a new telecommunications infrastructure. They go into their network, and they provision you. Rather, they configure your services for the set of requested capabilities. Essentially, you get a telecommunications system configured to your needs, which will differ from that of other customers, although it was built on the same common infrastructure.

We have adopted a very similar model for our commerce platform. In the perfect world of the future, we can bring a business on board, get them connected to our network, and provide them with a custom set of services. They interact with the trading partners they wish to interact with, based on a common, shared infrastructure. When we get to this perfect world, that is the model we see. Implementing this model requires a specific architecture in terms of how the technologies are assembled.

Ultimately, this presents very significant barriers to entry. It requires a lot of intellectual property, strategic thinking, and design you can't buy off the shelf. We expect to gain strategic advantage in the way we put these communities together, the model we've used to assemble it, and the intellectual property that goes into building it, which takes a lot of time and money for a competitor to try to duplicate. We believe that because we have put all the pieces together, we are in the best position to leverage the end result. Trying to duplicate that kind of infrastructure and intellectual property remains very difficult.

F.R. (Frank) Campagnoni is the chief technology officer of GE Global eXchange Services, a global leader in business-to-business electronic commerce. His role is to define and drive GXS's technology strategy in support of the company's objective to be the premier provider of supply-chain solutions.

Mr. Campagnoni is a recognized expert in business-to-business electronic commerce. He contributes to and is frequently quoted in trade periodicals. He has been an active participant in industry standards consortia, such as the Object Management Group, and served on the Managing Board of RosettaNet, a consortium of information technology supply-chain partners. He was recognized by

InfoWorld magazine as one of the 25 most influential CTOs in 2001 and top CTO for 2001 in the Web services category.

Mr. Campagnoni has been a leader in the design, construction, and deployment of network-centric business solutions for more than 15 years, encompassing client/server, distributed object, and Internet technologies. He played a role in the development of a number of seminal networking technologies and holds two patents for his work in distributed object technology.

Joining GE Global eXchange Services in June 1998, Mr. Campagnoni earlier held senior management and technical positions with AT&T Solutions, IBM, and Sun Microsystems and was a professor of computer science at Northeastern University in Boston.

Executive Reports

Targeted Reports Written by Hundreds of C-Level Executives

Executive Reports: How to Get an Edge as a CTO

This insider look at succeeding as a CTO and technology professional is written by C-Level executives (CEOs, CFOs, CTOs, CMOs) from the world's leading companies. Each executive shares their knowledge on how to get an edge in business, from managing your technology resources to continuing to learn in your field to understanding other areas in your company better (such as marketing, finance, operations, hr). Pulling from every book, report and journal published by Aspatore Books, also covered are over 250 specific, proven innovative strategies and methodologies practiced by leading executives and technology professionals that have helped them gain an edge. This report is designed to give you insight into the leading executives of the world, and assist you in developing additional "special skills" that can help you be even more successful as a technology professional. Also included in this report is a special section written by Mark Minevich, former CTO of IBM, on the job responsibilities and resources a CTO needs to be successful. $279 – 120 Pages, 8.5 x 11

Executive Reports: Selling Software to Top U.S. Companies & Industries

This insider look at over 30 major industries and professions is the ideal tool for software executives and salespeople who need to "get smart fast" before a client meeting, sales pitch or other event. Each industry overview has sections written by current, leading C-Level executives (CEOs, CFOs, CTOs, CMOs, Partners) from their respective industries and enables you to speak intelligently with anyone after being "briefed" by a leading executive from that industry. In addition, the book includes parts written by leading CTOs from Global 500 Companies on the types of products, solutions and software that they are looking for to help them succeed. The report is now a "how to sell software report," but rather a report that enables you to understand an industry's/company's pain in order to better sell your products/services. Over 200 executives from Global 1000 companies such as GE, Amex, Coke, AT&T, Duke Energy and companies from every other major industry have contributed to this brief. This report also includes a special section on sales ethics and dealing with clients/prospective clients according to new industry standard ethical guidelines. Pulling from every book, report and journal published by Aspatore, Executive Reports are the best way to get an edge and get smart fast on particular industries and topics. $549 – 800 Pages

TECHNOLOGY BOOKS
Visit Your Local Bookseller Today or www.Aspatore.com For More Information

OTHER BEST SELLERS

- <u>Term Sheets & Valuations</u> – A Line by Line Look at the Intricacies of Term Sheets & Valuations, 100 Pages, $14.95

- <u>Deal Terms</u> – The Finer Points of Deal Structures, Valuations, Term Sheets, Stock Options and Getting Deals Done, 240 Pages, $49.95

- <u>Corporate Ethics</u> – The Business Code of Conduct for Ethical Employees, 160 Pages, $14.95

- <u>The Governance Game</u> – Restoring Boardroom Excellence & Credibility in America, 128 Pages, $24.95

- <u>Inside the Minds: The Ways of the VC</u> - VCs from Polaris, Bessemer, Venrock, Mellon Ventures & More on Identifying Opportunities, Assessing Business Models & Establishing Valuations, 220 Pages, $27.95

- <u>The Golf Course Locator for Business Professionals</u> – Golf Courses Closest to Largest Companies, Law Firms, Cities & Airports, 180 Pages, $12.95

- <u>Business Travel Bible</u> – Must Have Phone Numbers, Business Resources & Maps, 240 Pages, $14.95

- <u>Living Longer, Working Stronger</u> – Simple Steps for Business Professionals to Capitalize on Better Health, 160 Pages, $14.95

- <u>Business Grammar, Style & Usage</u> – Rules for Articulate and Polished Business Writing and Speaking, 100 Pages, $14.95

- <u>ExecRecs</u> – Executive Recommendations For The Best Business Products & Services, 140 Pages, $14.95

- <u>Executive Adventures</u> – 50+ Exhilarating Out of the Office Escape Vacations, 100 Pages, $14.95

- <u>The C-Level Test</u> – Business IQ & Personality Test for Professionals of All Levels, 60 Pages, $17.95

- <u>The Business Translator</u> – Business Words, Phrases & Customs in Over 65 Languages, 540 Pages, $29.95